A NEW BEGINNING

A NEW BEGINNING

BY

KWAME DAWES AND JOHN KINSELLA

PEEPAL TREE

First published in Great Britain in 2018
Peepal Tree Press Ltd
17 King's Avenue
Leeds LS6 1QS
UK

ISBN 13: 9781845234249

Supported using public funding by
ARTS COUNCIL
ENGLAND

INDEX OF FIRST LINES

All the odd-numbered poems are by John Kinsella (JK) and all the even-numbered poems are by Kwame Dawes (KD).

1.

Communication towers don't fill in the gaps.
Climbing to the heights from the Bindibindi-
Toodyay Road, or rising suddenly from Church
Gully Road, and seeing Babel gloating in its clearing,
tall as heck and brazen as a hotwire, dead fox
rotting on the shoulder, language loses
track of purpose. Whose purpose?
Some are delighted. We might spark
across the gap with greater clarity,
move faster. But I don't need that –
fast enough is fast enough. I can't
adjust hemispheres outside timeshift,
no meridian divisions between sides
of the brain. So I take to reading
(yet again, yet again) Hardy's
The Return of the Native
in an effort to calibrate
my unbelonging, and yet
fastidious attention to what's
preached and what's listened to
rouses the green in the grasslands
and tempers the black-shouldered kite's
watching. Truly, I hope it will be there
watching all suspiciously in the morning,
out over the frost's redactions.

JK

2.

After a photo by Anthony Hernandez

What do I return to? There is a dream
of a wall made of the thick bases
of coke bottles, a tantalising shelter
for the outdoor shower, terracotta
tiles that darken to blood when the water
spreads over it. Above, as if the limits
of this kiosk are the limits of peace,
is the sky, a lilac-tinged blue. I return
to nothing, really. This morning,
a storm gallivanted over the prairie,
lit up the windows, made the dog
whimper at our bedside, and on
the radio, a preacher spoke of Job's
unhelpful friends. I was awake,
and the distraction of a chaos
outside the limits of my peace
was enough. I am avoiding
the obvious hauntings – you heard,
I am sure, of the two men shot,
black men, the phone cameras,
the police, the fatigue of this,
how hard it is to start again
to say that something is not right,
how hard it is to consider
the alternative: we live
in a land of guns, so people
will die from gunshot wounds.
Why is this remarkable?
Why all the protests?
The truth is I slept through
the storm, dreaming of
that shower in Treasure Beach

where, naked, and speckled
with the spray of water, I stared
at the limits of freedom,
above my cooling head.

KD

3.

I am a child obsessed with guns.

I am a child coveting an air rifle and targets that will pop up on cue.

I am a child stalking the wandoo bushlands with my uncle's farm weapon on the lookout for birds outside the coop.

I am a child in a room full of model warplanes and heavy armour and terrain models of battle fields.

I am a child reading Walt Whitman's "Drum Taps" on the edge of the Chapman Valley where explorers conjured and met war parties.

I am a child watching *To Sir With Love* and piecing together a world I am not part of but feel I am part of in some way.

I am a child in my adult body wanting gun manufacturers to see the errors of their ways, to rise out of the pools of blood they've dished up.

I am a child in my adult body wanting guns to leave equations of hate and leave not just one last man standing but all people talking even arguing.

I am a child in my adult body who marches for peace and who wants all living things to live and wonders how the child can be the man.

I am a child in my adult body who wants Before Common Era to be where crimes of hate and violence reside and all now is after and peaceful.

I am a child in my adult body who sees the fairground ducks plinked and downed on their conveyor belts to be hauled back for more and more.

I am a child in my adult body who would rewrite rules of engagement and relegate "strategy" and "tactics" to metaphors for gardening.

JK

4.

(i)

You learn the sombre weight of a 303,
after drills with the wooden imitation,
crudely painted black and white;
you learn that mastery comes
from the wrist and forearm strength
to hold the barrel with index
finger and thumb, then flick
on command, feel it airborne
for that instance of precision,
before the slap of right palm against
the magazine, the barrel pressed snug
between arm and chest, before
the quick slashing return
of the left arm to the side.
There is power in this,
though you know these rifles,
trucked to the campsite
with nonchalant buck private
escorts from Up Park Camp,
have been fixed-up,
rendered impotent. But you
learn how to break that tool
apart, clean its elements,
polish its parts, and you
see how simple its genius is,
how death can be as ordinary
as a fountain pen, a typewriter,
the hand-press turning pulp
into lumpy sheets of raw paper.

(ii)

Once, they told me, a gunman
waved his fat black pistol over me
like a priest swinging his chalice,
and they were all praying
I would not wake up and startle him,
as he was sweating with fear,
and when I did, we all laughed
for the gunman was gone,
and we were still alive.

(iii)

The starter's pistol, they said,
fired blanks, but it was Captain
who told me which box of shells to bring
from his roach-dusty office drawers
and so I knew what it could do,
and so each blow of its report –
before the sprinters ran helter-
skelter along the dusty track
lined with asphalt, while the crowd
shouted and mimicked jockeys
whipping, whipping, whipping –
would fill my stomach with a heavy
weight of nausea, the terror
before desire, the water-limbed
weakness I carry in my body
these days, moving through
a city in which all the neighbours
are rehearsing their moment
before the camera. "This kind
of thing never happens here,
never happens here at all."

KD

5.

Today, we decide to sort our grocery shopping
in Northam, taking in a walk around the river
to make something special of the occasion.

The river is alive, which it isn't always,
and winter rains are caught in the paradox
of flushing through and introducing

farm chemicals in the expanse before the town,
the expanse before the weir where it starts
its tumble down through the hills to the coast.

White swans, of that colony struggling to stay
viable, stretch high on their small island nesting
ground. A beautiful irony in a world where

"pioneers" tried to bend symbolism to their own
gain. Then we rest and Tim reads his book
set in ancient Rome – a family who have offended

the emperor on their way to Roman Britain
to start again. He is deft with all ironies, Tim,
and as he tells me about it, the pock pock pock

of gunfire. The firing range on the edge of town
is heating up. I tell Tim the red flag will be out –
red rag of the bulls. He says it makes him so sick

he can't read. Irony can't sustain everything.
Driving back home the "long way", we pass
the red flag dangling like bloodshed, a rag

around a wound that's flapped free, and see
a pair of young men in camouflage gear walking
along the edge of the road. They stare us down,

one carrying a pistol case, swinging it back
and forth like a school satchel, daring us to twitch.
You cannot "bear arms" in Australia, but walking

home in a country town from the range
the contents of a case are conjecture. The rise
of the far right in this country barely shelters

behind party names like One Nation or Shooters
and Fishers Party, or Australian Patriots – they feel close
to the America of now. They swagger

with rights, make amendments in their heads
for all of us. The river flows by the shooting range,
rich with chemical fallout, out in the country.

JK

6.

This low-bellied cloud cover
over Lincoln surprises me –
the air is muggy, and a strange
foreboding comfort settles.

In the novel I will never write
it is the last day of their meeting
though they do not know it,
but this is the opening scene of the book,
and after this the deaths begin.

The couple arrives in the tree-full courtyard,
a ritual repeated each weekday
for a decade, though for festival season,
and the feast days, they've stayed away.

They wait for the teasing accidents
of the unseen pianist – always an open chord
not in the same key, and then a quick
wayward arpeggio in the higher notes.

Then the full composition, full bodied,
a nameless air, though they never
speak, so all they offer are smiles.
Who knows what the other knows?

The couple dances – in the novel, they have
danced for ten years, a man and a woman,
nameless, voiceless, just two bodies
seeking assurance in the ritual.

Here, in this moment of the book,
the piano is silent. They stare
at the balcony – the curtain flaps
as usual, but no sound, no music.

Then a portly woman with a bandana,
carrying a heavy rug, steps out, looks down
and smiles. She never existed before.
She drapes the rug over the railing.

It is Persian, curlicues of blue and red,
epics unfolding in the soft light.
The couple look away, embarrassed;
she leaves first, he follows.

The rest is the world collapsing in,
a city regulated by guns,
leaders betraying leaders,
money changing hands,

wars, and rumours of wars,
snowfall in the summer,
a veritable feast for the poets
who have mastered the Jeremiads

of doom. It was always this way
for them, the man and the woman;
the courtyard was their shelter
of deep secrets – the kind that accumulate

over years and years to become
a monument of betrayals;
though nothing happens,
everything happens,

for in a time of calamity
while a nation folds in and starts
to feast on its own innards –
so much blood, so little peace –

every instant of peace, every escape
into music is an act of abandonment,
every poem a deep sin, every brush-stroke
a betrayal, every silence a wounding.

On a day as grey as this, the end
of things seems imminent. Lincoln's
skies are wide as the prairie; the naked
eye cannot see the limits of this gloom.

I think of this novel of deep silence
as a way not to think of those waking
to bury their violently dead,
that heavy searching for a narrative

of anger to allow them to face
the day. When my father died suddenly,
I sought out the villains quickly,
they kept me company for years,

they gave me anger for sorrow,
they gave me the stoic seething a son
of a dead, old campaigner should bear;
they gave me reason to replace

the incomprehensible. Tomorrow,
I will protest the infestation of guns,
but today, I sit in the shelter of this
city's darkening morning

and contemplate the choices of fiction,
as in who returns the next day,
the man or the woman? I know
one will not. I still can't tell which.

KD

19

7.

I was going to write yesterday evening
after making the discovery, but put it off
to think over your poem, Kwame, your
unwritten or never-to-be written novel.

In the meantime, the killings in Nice.
And the many killings elsewhere.
And the news that the State government
here has managed to have an environmental

ruling protecting wetlands overturned
in a court of appeal – they claim license
to send the bulldozers in, to make more
freeway. The skies here are so often

sullied blue with burning and the sick
reflections of "clearing". Will I ever see
the prairies of your setting? I will hear
a piano as Tim practices for his Sunday

lesson with his nanna. Music resonating.
The discovery. The article is everything.
So much ill-will towards "nature" here
that realisations of Aeschylus-like cruelty

is not uncommon. But last evening I went
to close the top gate before the climb back
downhill, I noticed a plastic bag flapping
on top of an ant colony. Investigating,

I found a half-portion of desiccated coconut
in the torn bag, clearly tossed from the quiet
roadside onto the cones and clearing
of the antworld which connects via paths

with other antworlds around the valley.
Desiccated coconut mixed with ant poison –
an alluring treat, a compulsion to add to winter
stores, an enticement and a trigger to latent activity.

Bonanza. Death in the tunnels. The curling
bodies in luminous pitchblack. Sensory city failure.
Necropolis. Larvae aloneness. Message betrayal.
Mimicry of surfaceworld. And the tossing,

the hurling of the poison into the zone we occupy,
where our son walks and shows an interest
in all things, especially the beloved ants
he's watched over for year after year,

in all seasons. This narrative is different
yet familiar. The antagonists are invisible
and witless to puns. If you hear them yell
it's an abrupt yawp. The America

that remains in him isn't of guns,
and the Whitman he holds in reserve
is focalised through Langston Hughes
who runs like a river through him,
        a confluence.

JK

21

8.

This morning, I envy my old friend the physicist,
a thought-companion thirty years ago,
sandalled, thin cotton cariba shirt,
floppy 1950s trousers, his head a-bob,
his mouth constantly going. He never
vacillated at the cafeteria, three crisp-
skinned golden dumplings, a mess of eggs
scrambled and fluffy, a ritual, and he would
eat with that quick impatience of a man
with things to do, places to go. We talked
of Plato and Jesus Christ; Paul, the saint,
has become this paper-skinned man in my head,
his sins neatly arranged in the clean logic
of the dead and the living, his heavy hand
of correction, and the surprise in how tender
his wailing at the altar seemed. I write as if
he is dead, but he isn't. The man I envy
is not that fledgling youth pretending to be
a man – he was a virgin then, and his heart
had only been shattered once, and righteousness
grew in him like untamed kudzu, verdant,
vegetable, relentless. Now he is a father,
and he trains his sons in the art
of weapons, though they live on an island
for which the terrorists have yet no language.
Yet, in this world in which all barrios
are world markets, all kraals, thoroughfares,
with his laptop, the static magic of symbols
multiplying in the air, he is the prophet
I envy. The world, he says is a simple
place, and the blueprint of prophecy
is laid out for all to see. I have stopped
reading him after calamities, because
he leaves my terror, my deep fears,

my bewilderment deeper-seated,
and I feel a fool for not knowing
what to do with a truck hurtling
through a street and crushing the bones
of a hundred people – dead, all gone,
just like that. He has an answer
for that, I am sure. And were I to ask
what to do with the news of that dread-locked
Castile with his forty traffic tickets and fines,
and his four bullet holes, and his body
a blooming fountain of red filling
our screens, his woman, his child,
what of this? Were I to wonder
why my son's shaved head, after
his failure to tame the locks he wore
for a year, leaves me relieved; were I
to ask why I seek shelter in language,
in the trivial narratives of invented
people, he would, I am sure, offer me
the wisdom of the ages. I know he thinks
that the beast slouching towards
DC this fall is the gift of a merciful God,
and I suffer for not having the strength
to debate, the strength to push back;
for not saying, "Your island of thought
is your sanctuary, my friend. You have
built a bunker of inscrutable logic,
and the players will always dance
your dance, and the world will end
as it must end, and maybe this is
the age of the games we play
on the screens, click – a killing, click –
a cache of gifts or bombs, click – another
life, click – game over, only to begin again."
And even this is not enough,
because I do love him, and he is still

the man eating scrambled eggs and laughing,
and I am watching in wonder and joy. John,
you have haunted me with those tunnels,
those alarmed ants, that apocalypse
of unsuspecting disaster – this is no metaphor,
and yet it is, at least in the way
it settles its meaning on me.
To think there is a pure America
is my el dorado – I will keep looking,
for I, too, have seen hints of it,
or maybe I am just too tired to see.
To think Whitman's stroll through the city
of New York is repeated by Langston Hughes,
to think this is true is a bunker of hope,
but I know Langston's "I, Too" was youthful
hope, this before the lynchings grew too many,
this before the scrutiny of the agents,
this before the Montage of a Dream Deferred.
They break you, they break you. Yesterday,
I read of a Jamaican man called Garnette Cordogan,
pushing hard against dry scepticism with an aspirant
lyric of the walking people – the night walkers
of cities, those who are the canaries
in the mine of a nation's civility and freedom.
He longed to be Mr. Whitman, to follow
his footsteps through that great city,
but we know the revelations a black
body learns, as sure as this world
repeats its truths: "What no one
had told me," he writes, "was that I
was the one who would be considered
a threat." Such an ordinary thing
to say. And I grew dumb in the way
that we must go wordless to meaning –
I stopped thinking. Maybe that is when
I thought of my friend, that is when

I longed for his simple logic, his equations
of the end of time – the villains
and the heroes, the wheat and the tare.
Still, I knew that to expect comfort from him
would be like the days spent waiting
for a book to arrive in the mail,
a book pregnant with a meaning
I only suspect will be there. "Todavía
no ha llegado aquí," I want to say.
"Todavía estoy esperando."

KD

9.

How we find our way out of siege places.
How we renegotiate the terms of belonging
we live by – the warped social contract,
the taxpayer-funded big stick, the business
shunt into pragmatic service, the multinational
largesse of a product known as a cross-cultural utopia
that addresses each demographic, markets
to each scenario, and still squeezes profit to the top.

Here, it's a dictatorship of neighbours, Kwame,
a bullying from the earliest cries in the clinic
receiving immunisations, to the array of school-
control mechanisms, to the ragging at voting
booths to do as we do, do as we say. Some years
ago I received a message from a boy – a man – who'd
been in the same year as me at high school and had
joined in with the jocks who blocked a corridor
with school bags, hemmed me in and bashed me.
My friend W., who is now an inventor in LA,

the youngest ever graduate of the University of WA,
was the only one who expressed his disgust. But
the bully (not the worst of them by any stretch)
had found God and was repenting. What could
I say? Move on? I am – we are? – marked by
each incident. But that's the way of it. This moving on.
As an aside, a few years ago my friend W.
contacted me out of the blue, and every
now and again we swap emails. I exchanged
only the one with my repentant persecutor,
though as he vanished back into the data of life,
I wished him well. His long, slow form of suffering.
For me, he was one of many, one incident
in a narrative of "difference" and consequences.

W. suffered as well. We never mention
any of it in our brief emails across the world.

And so it has been pouring and pouring here,
unlike anything we've seen for decades. River,
streams and brook are breaking banks, paddocks
flooding. Spoonbills and white-faced herons
are reclaiming ground lost to the poetics of dust
year in year out. Ring-necked parrots of green
bellies and yellow bellies are messing with divisions
of subspecies in the liquefaction, in the riot of water.
The land is eroding fast and bending to a forgotten will.
The shooters will be cock-a-hoop. Doomsday
is their revelation, their expectation, so even
if the damaged world flourishes, they will
be in their element as we rapidly revert to dust.

JK

10.

for W.S. Merwin

The old poet plants trees. He long abandoned
the regime of punctuation – breath, he said,
was found in the ordering of thought, and he
was learned enough to have traced the history
of those markers, prudent enough to know
that all punctuation seeks first to mark
breath and the shape of meaning.
The trees are orphans, the last of so many
tribes, and he finds a empty place,
stares at the line of the river from the spot,
and imagines meaning the way the dying
imagine a future without them. When
he sees the tiny window of deep blue
and shine of the water from his vantage,
he plants and every gesture is an elegy
for himself. This is how he mourns
his life, this is how he laments the passing
of his body. The earth is soft with rain
on this nursery, and his lines are careless,
though he says only a foolish husbandman
of trees imagines he knows the order
of things. Beneath the soil, where roots
bore their way into their network
of entanglements, there is where the deep
unknowable resides. The poet hobbles as fast
as his body will let him between the tree
trunks, moving as if he carries in his trail
the string that will lead him home. The poet
is not of this country, but knows his bones
will be buried in this dark soil, where
the heat and all its breeding parasites
will welcome him to the heavy clay.

All imagining is flight – not in the way
of the soaring, but in the way of escape,
a kind departure with no promise
of return. The old poet is not my friend,
and yet it is he who I think of as the body
moving through this tropic humidity,
daily walking his last, and still content
with the ritual of tree planting. There is
faith in this. The trees will outlive him,
and this blunt truth is a kind of immortality,
the seed of it, anyway. And in this invention,
I am learning the magic of flight – leaving
the impolite suburbs for a rain-soaked landing
so far up-river that its surface is black
as polished augite from the silt of centuries
of dead things. In this silence all actions
will heal the bruises I carry; this is what
I imagine to be the inheritance willed
to me by the limping, tree-planting poet.

KD

11.

Without shape and vernacular
I am left with a full palette of colour.

Naturally, I am hesitant. I lack the polish
of cafe life, and have to quash the extrusive

poem rising with the magma. It's a risk,
but I am a risk taker. Bound up in paradox.

Language is a grab bag I should be wary of.
I am never wary enough. The "mind the gap"

warnings in the tube station didn't prevent
me from slipping onto the tracks, between

the wheels. I can be as liquid. I process
anxiety under trees where limbs have

occasionally come crashing to the ground.
These limbs rest where they fall or burn

in a slow combustion stove. I see vast realms
of wheat as oceans that have been tackled

by navigators greedy for knowledge and wealth.
I know what life is for the wheat seed from woe to go.

Retreating further, I think about collations of moss
on the Mizen and Beara peninsulas, and the moss

here accruing and moving slowly outwards
under the acacias with short lifespans up near

the granite boulders. I want to translate or
create a version of Annette von Droste-Hülshoff's

"Im Moose" – all that moss in thick shade,
the slightly dull light I read by each night.

But I need shape. I need a vernacular
of some sort. I have an abundance

of untouched colour to paint
into a form that will resolve itself.

JK

12.

There is a goshawk. There is a falconer.
There are chunks of flesh, there are
strips of bleeding flesh, muscles and grizzle;
there is a bloodied beak; there are hedges,
stretches of organised countryside,
wild bramble, heavy clouds, grey skies,
poplars leaning, woods dense as caves,
narrow lanes, a woman running, panting,
her face bleeding, her eyes searching
the sky, searching the tree-line, desperate
for some sign of the goshawk. She is the falconer,
she is mourning a dead father, she is consumed
by grey, she is heavy with her own sweat,
her body neglected, her mind smoky;
she never cries, but wakes each day
with her chest full of stones, and all
of this follows me as a shadow, as I
walk the streets of my sunny city,
and a voice traces the path of what
the impolite must call madness.
She is touched, she is giddy with blood-
thirst, she feeds this goshawk flesh,
she lets her fingers dry with blood.
This is how I remember it, this is how
a body submits itself to its creature-self,
how a body withdraws into the grime
of routine when all that matters is the ritual
of feeding, shitting, sleep, and the claw
and blood of sublime flight. This is all,
this is the cave language builds for
us, as if here we may abandon the chaos
of the world about us. I know that,
given the right horrors, we can turn
into creatures consumed by the most
basic of desires, creatures who arrive

at peace by violent denial. But this
is a luxury, and I carve out my dumb
silences in daily pockets – a voice
unfolding the narrative of animal
fantasy, a woman's decline into beast,
before I rise out of it, and face the due
preparations for the fall, when this
world will test all resolve. This I know,
as I know that the house, her cage,
is a few chains from the chapel
where she can kneel to pray so deeply,
and from the broad windows of
her cottage, she can see the spire,
while she walks through the house
naked, her hair a chaotic cacophony,
her springy walk, a body moving
across open spaces as if the eyes
on her are her true shelter. All exposed
madness is its own escape; a naked
body, once it forgets the limits of clothes,
turns invisible in the bright light
(and this and what follows is the necessary
fantasy that haunts me long
after the story ends, with the mute
understatement of the studious lyric),
her eyes holding in the dark, until
a stench as violent as rotting flesh,
loose shit, the sour of vomit, a stench
of sweating crowds, the ground
dark with old blood and the flies,
the sluggish flies circling – the scent
of the slowly dying fills her nostrils;
and as she retches, as her mouth fills
with water, she thinks of the fading
light, the hawk and spit of the stragglers,
and the lingering stench of grace.

KD.

13.

I don't recognise the raptor
in Robinson Jeffers' "Rock and Hawk".
Most days here we see black-shouldered kites

and sometimes brown hawks and peregrine falcons,
and, in bouts, the great circling wedge-tailed eagles
which deep-survey the valley for prey.

When we visit my brother
in my old high school town of Geraldton
far up the west coast, sea eagles

nest in a crow's nest made from an opened cray pot
mounted on a stylus opposite the Point Moore
lighthouse – flashing out over the breakers

of Hell's Gate where tiger sharks rake the reefs. An emblem?
Of persistence against all odds? Though protected
by law, law is a victim of money and fear,

and here the eagle-shooters ensure
their acts are cloistered. Stories of longevity
and powers outside the body aren't mine

to latch on to, and I won't. For me, there's
nothing mystical about any raptor presence,
about the arc or fall or strike of their hunt.

It's a world outside the human, which isn't
to say that for some the auguries and ramifications
aren't co-ordinates in their lives, and the lives

of community. But I know how an image
can be bent to the needs of its maker, how originality
and the inflections of self might merge

stories that clash in all other respects.
Respect. The bird. Yes, and the stories. Creation.
The bird and its rodent or reptile or mammal or bird

victim. When I was thirteen I knew a boy
who hooded a falcon, who kept it bound to his arm.
He showed the paraphernalia of controlling

"the wild" at school. It excited him. He told
of a controlling and wild and fertile future.
He could describe this in poetic ways,

though he claimed poetry meant nothing
to him. But I am looking for no intermediary
between my all-too-human state, my status.

Stark realism? Inclination to documentary?
Action without judgement? Witness?
I've never noticed a raptor "hang"

in the sky – when stilled in air
they are always
on the move.

JK

14.

It is like writing history with lightning,
and my only regret is that it is all so terribly true.

— Woodrow Wilson, 1915

Reverend Dixon was beyond himself. One rag
called him triumphant at the news of the monumental
popularity of the film. This is the century of big things,
he would have thought, knowing that somewhere up there,
where all scale is calibrated against the hubris
of man's capacity to build swaying buildings, big
things, like this monumental film — "thirty miles
of filth", Du Bois griped — all that lightning streaking
across the hungry corneas; this has to be a holy thing,
something that eclipsed the papyrus scroll, the lamb-
skin inked with the eternal Holy Writ — this illumination
cutting through the air and magicking into being
bodies, mountains, horses, fields. This is akin
to the finger on the wall, and perhaps we must
not blame old Woodrow for being caught up
in the moment, in the amazement of it all,
for he could not have known the greasy
mechanics of capturing light and turning
it all into a grand alchemy; nor would he have
known, until Dixon's triumphant jig and holy twirl,
that the reverend sought to conjure a new
world order into being: "The real purpose
of my film was to revolutionise Northern
audiences that would transform every man
into a Southern partisan for life."
Here in the cool Northwest, where the Sound
offers the last vestiges of a continent before
the stretch of endless water, if you look
away from the clapboard houses and quaint

36

corner stores, out to the water, where you can
discern the ghost of Mount Ranier in the sky,
it is possible to imagine that the old growth
trees do outlive us, and our tiny complaints
and prophecies of carnage are whisperings
like the swirl of the wind off the water.
The wars will come, the dead will shout
from the grave, and still, we may well forget
it all, as we are wont to do. Joe, my fine
poet friend, with his whiskers like a Roman
olive grower in midsummer, looks with
earnest at me and says, "He is going to lose
so bad it is going to be embarrassing."
And we all long to believe, though today
I remembered old Woodrow, who did not lose,
but he too came and went, and left us
with two sobering truths – that the castle
can be ruled by the feckless, or worse, and still stand;
that even as a man curses all that is good,
he sometimes manages to speak in the language of
holy angels – "writing history with lightning".
Ahh, indeed, indeed. Even the slouching beast
will speak with honey on his lips. This is his
true terror, the sweetest honey on his tongue.

KD

15. capacitor

I was struck by lightning twice as a child
and have had near misses on three or four
occasions. Lightning has written itself
into me and I can't get rid of it. Maybe
I look at history slant because of this.
Walking the port where I fell, fell
night closed in on me. Not the open
spaces where lightning found me first,
but street corners, buildings and wharfs
sensing a fractured spark, a wrongly stored
electricity that drove me to wander,
homeless, when I didn't need to be.
Streets laid out like the circuit board
of an old transistor radio, its power
source the harbour plus a storm violent
overhead. I was drawn to the dark ships
but no passage was offered. I was lost.

JK

16.

And there is the sin of the prophetess –
a hazard of the art of seeing – the capacity
to roll out the wisdom of sayings
secreted deep inside the powdered
cleavage of old mothers, or tucked behind
the ears of carpenters whose arthritic
fingers still manage to know the grain
of wood with familiar, almost instinctual
ease. "Not everything what good
fe talk, good fe eat." The prophetess wants
to talk and eat the scroll. The prophetess
delights in the pleasures of words
slipping over her tongue, the lightning
strike of shocking, fleeting artistry
against the tumult and hurl of clouds,
steel grey, deep mauve, moaning black.
This is what the prophetess understands,
and even she is shocked at the sweet
symmetry of revelation. But it is
in the eating of things, the consumption
of the pretty little morsels, what with
their aroma and heat and colour,
it is in the eating that we know the truth
of this saying. The prophetess will ignore
her own advice, and this is her downfall.
So much that comes in dreams, must
stay in dreams. So much that arrives
in revelation, must settle in revelation.
So much that arrives in the secret place
of our art, must stay hidden in the secret
place of that art. And this is what the prophetess
cannot abide, for the prophetess is made
to anthem all news, and this is the downfall
of prophecy. She knows that where seeing

happens, where the smoke rising from
the bones takes shape like the magic
of lenticular clouds hovering over the city,
she knows that this place is bramble thick,
and stinks of the warm, seething excretions
of the body. It is the place of wounding
and aches, it is where the hems of all garments
are stained with the basic morass of our
living and dying, and it is here that the tray
arrives with the delights – how can she not
devour? How can she turn away? Is this
not what she is made to do? Of course,
I have long felt her reshaping my body.
Thirty years ago, a stranger saw my legs dangling
from a balcony; he then came closer
until he saw my body, and face, and I
saw in his eyes the shocked betrayal of himself,
how he had imagined me a woman.
He shouted, "Dutty batty-bwai!" and
hurried away, as if chased off by the words
of a screaming prophetess. I have grown
the breasts of the prophetess, and soon
I will sit in that bone-yard and eat the sweets
offered as she would. Such a long way of saying,
it is I who contemplates here the hazards of our art.

KD

17.

(i)

Bereft. Wanting to hear speech
written in the eye of the well
where reflections are brief
and can't take. Broken
to quench even a winter
thirst. Foresee or waver.

(ii)

Yes, these quartz crystals
are large and slow under
the brief, lowish sun.
And over there? Pyrites,
but fool's gold camouflaged
by the seepage of earlier rains:
the hillside profile at work.

(iii)

Caught in nomenclature failure
the weapons manufacturers
gloat filmically. Directors
of our mutual documentary.
IN or OUT of the club,
the same wounds
will be wondered
over in the grave,
the incinerator,
the crucible.

(iv)

Slogan rebound.
Cloister, piazza,
royal enclaves.
Parks with hunting
rights. Passive-
aggressive learning
tools. Here: an old fashioned
photo album. Circa.

JK

18.

It is as if all monumental effort
to manage the chaos of knowing,
the madness of an archive
that consumes all things
(without discrimination,
swallowing, swallowing),
as if the years spent by cloistered
scribes to make narratives
that we may digest all those
lovely fictions, those orderly
histories, those sermons,
those canons laid out
in alphabetical order –
oh the assurance of this,
the comfort of this –
it is as if, sudden so,
with no rhyme and no reason,
it has all been taken away,
and we are left on our own,
bewildered and free, free, free.
This is how I define "the news",
this is the delusion of knowing
in a house with no walls,
no doors, no windows,
just a wind filled with voices.
I understand now why
this country welcomes
the crude efficiency
of the arrogant demigod;
why we tailor the world
to suit what we do not know;
why we are so tired, so tired,
so brainweary, why it is futile
to say, "Think, think, think…"

I say "we" to grant authority
to this "wisdom", but I mean me,
I mean I, I mean I know
that on mornings like this,
there is a fatigue that remains;
and I long for the album
that cabins my life tidily:
here is where we begin,
here is where it ends,
and these are the sorrows,
and these are the joys,
and this is delight,
and this is horror,
and this is all labelled,
dated, filed in columns
of roots, in columns
of platoons. Well, that was
a lovely delusion, I say,
and the truth is – flat
on my back, my head
on the earth – I can hear
the shifting plates.
This is bigger than us,
and yet smaller than us,
too, and here is the end
of fatigue. We know that
the feasts of currency
are never neutral,
and though tedious,
this thinking, it is what
we do, how we are made.
Our fictions are never tidy,
but the lines bring clarity,
and this is something – I like to say.

KD

19.

We all have our stock epithets
as means of survival, I guess.
Mine, at the moment, is: so much
is overdetermined. The so much
is the variable, the ambiguity,
the fill-in-this-space with "world",
the "here and now", what will come,
certainly what has been. But last night,
returning late from our expedition
to the city where Tim has his
Goethe Society German class,
a new path in the maze of certainty
and stock epithets was offered,
and I am running with it.
We always watch carefully
during the long drive home
from the city, searching fringes
on the edge of headlights for roos
ready to leap over dark roads – an impact
as endgame. You'd know this,
Kwame, as we knew it too living
in the States, that a deer-strike
alters destiny for human and deer.
So, too, an impact with a kangaroo.
It messes with the left and right sides
of the brain, and with the cells themselves.
The absurdity of metal and flesh.
It doesn't balance the equation.
We saw none during the long stretches
when we expected to. But almost home,
a large boomer leapt across the road,
strafed by headlights – even anti-hunters,
even pacifists, even animal libbers
such as ourselves, wield a deadly weapon

when driving. Lethal force. The right
to bear an unstoppable reality. World events
subtext everything we write in our
specific localities, this interconnectedness
of causality. Tracy called 'Roo!' in time
and I pulled up, and it made its way
into the bush. We turned into our driveway
grateful it was only a close call, but mainly
thinking that things are not as overdetermined
as I've been saying. Hunters had been through
and wiped out the large roo mobs that move
here over the year. But there's a return,
a coming back on moonless nights
when the Milky Way lights
a different way, a different epic,
a glow to abstract thought.

JK

20.

There is the metaphor of the imagination
as a sort of untouched canvas, and madness
is the impetus to cover that emptiness
with the news we want to hear. In an
older voice, something as old as Spain
after the Moors, there is a kind of humour
in the meticulous ordering of things – the ordinary
man becoming a knight errant, and how
easily a journey becomes its own
glorious flight from the news. I am
finding myself making fictions in my head,
like this one of a man, who has a windfall
(I am still working on the nature of the thing:
money, Powerball – too random; a day
at the track – too specific; a grand book deal –
too temptingly easy to turn this into
the muddy paths of autobiography).
Still, there is a family, and a world,
and the tyranny of expectations,
and important, too, is the date: November
8th, and this is the same man who,
twelve years ago, saw a man rolled
out on a stretcher and was filled
with envy. Let's say he is older now,
and far less morose, so he sets his life
in order, discards his laptop and cell-
phone, packs a bag of basic things,
and avoids every wind of news
until he has managed to depart
his old world, and arrive in a small
town in Poland, or somewhere where
a black man needs a reason to be –
but once spoken to, every one in the old
hamlet of stone and steeples will know,

and none will question him. And there
he spends four years as if a monk,
avoiding all news of the world,
counting the hours by the light,
and consuming the fictions of civilisations:
no deaths, no new lives, and only
the handwritten letters he writes
to his blind mother, to be read by
Marva Jones, the slow-moving helper,
who sends back painstakingly written
reports on his mother's complaints.
One imagines how it must be
to re-enter a world after so many years
of silence, no wiser for it, no better
for having disappeared, and what
he sees is the novel I think to write.

KD

21.

My realworld is a shock of augmented loss.
No snapping of a scene into the eye of a phone,
no elimination of conjured ciphers of capitalism
warm and cuddly and vicious and myth-by-proxy.
Just thousands of acres of bush and forest mowed
down on this island continent every month.
Nothing left standing but cattle, bewildered
on their bare blankets, watching the edges
vanish. The closer they get, the further
they move away. No twistings of Tao
will bring energy or equanimity
or the substance of the Universe
to the ghostscapes grazier's lust for.
It's killing me. It's killing all of us,
but many if not most others seem not
to notice, or if they do, they shuffle
facts into the background. Our mortal
coil, the coil of a Caterpillar D9R bulldozer
("track-type tractor"), O holy ripper control lever,
O holy dual twist lever controls! Heavy
machinery which is what I hear now –
REALTIME – as a short while ago
I climbed the hill and looked out on a paddock
that wasn't there last year: no more echidnas,
no more roos, no more mulga snakes, no more
owls and tawny frogmouths and parrots nesting
in hollowed trees. Deleted. A green field
with a few sheep chewing into their destinies –
the "livestock transport" truck fuelling up
in town. That's it. Bald planet. All bad air
and blood. I hear the diesel engines
over the walls of valley – a fine winter's day –
and the sound changes the colour of the sky;
looking up I can see the moon and the stars

and planets orbiting them. Crystal clear.
A bright, low sun no interference.
No pollution interferes with my vision.

JK

22.

for Rick Black

At the pool he was stark, a runner's lines
of skin on bone, then the alarm of hair,
dark curls – the crown that Hebrew
poets search for the names of dark bushes
or cascading bundles of fruit or flowers
to describe. And then me, a circle
of indulgence, a tribe's substance, years
of building muscle under fat, an art,
a kind of joke. We would swim for an hour,
then leave the gym, eyes burning
from chlorine, our appetites grand,
and we would eat, counting calories,
he that he might add, me, that I might
lose. It has been twenty years since
our lunches in a café in steaming
Columbia, rehearsing each day
the slaughter of innocents, the blood
on the streets, the accounts of disaster.
He knew those streets during the Intifada,
saw the shells, the broken bodies,
the madness of dogma and history;
and I could recount the way of nations
unsettled by power hunger and the inebriation
from blood orgies. Daily, we would
recount, and then imagine a better time,
as if that myth were a possibility.
Still we laughed, deep guffaws,
and always, when the world seemed
to demand the reverence of silence,
we would think of poetry – first the way
we arrived at the truth of our complex
faiths – the quarrels with God, the art

of the unspoken deity – namelessness,
and yet so loudly present. The psalms,
the elegant psalms, became our repast –
he teaching me the secrets of the Hebrew
scripture, me unfolding the lyric
urgency of each fear, each hope, each
song. The hills, I know those hills,
not the barren stony places of Mt. Nebo,
but the graceful and densely green
Pisgah, deep in St. Elizabeth's hills
in Jamaica. As if in the hushed tones
of our talk, our heads leaning in together
we found prayer. He taught me
the simplicity of haikus through the chaotic
rendering of the city of Jerusalem
in morsels of terror and beauty. This
is friendship. It has been years now
since he left, and since our effort
to have lunches over words we have
grown, me rounder, he thinner,
and he has found a monkish craft
in the making of books, each letter
chosen for its promise of a certain
ordinary beauty. Yesterday, he wrote
to say that his book of translations
of Amichai's poems, with the motif
of windows, is now finished, and his
hands are stained with the inks
of making this book, each printing
following each printing, and he said,
it is a metaphor of us. He said it is
a metaphor of what we feared and
how what we feared – the rise of the beast,
the absurd comedy of tyrants, the crude
silence of God in the wind – this is what
Amichai translated is, a metaphor

for seeing our wrecked world while
sharing a salad of tomatoes and greens,
and long glasses of water, water.
Yesterday, too, someone tweeted
something I had written in a moment
of despair and hope, that "a love poem
written in a time of war is a political poem" –
which seems true these days, for I find
myself writing love poems in a time
of war. It seems that this is another
redundancy, like the letter, handwritten
on lined foolscap – so ordinary the gesture –
that this too, the choice of it, is an act
of love, and a political act, in these times
of monstrous beasts; which is all one can say
of what we do, John. It is love. How ordinary,
how remarkably and necessarily ordinary it is.

KD

23.

for Tracy

Yes, it is love, Kwame. And today is Tracy's
and my wedding anniversary, and she began
our day discussing the melodies of birds,
before we read further news of death
constructed out of death. It's the colours
of the earth that are ours, and not,
that take me to these geologies of script.

I have a remarkable book I treasure:
The Poetry of Kabbalah, translated
and edited by Peter Cole, and my
favourite page within the book is one
hundred and eighty five – a section page
but no divider – that simply says:

      Jewish Muslims

           *

      Muslim Jews

and in this page, and what unravels,
I find a hope or truth I can translate
into my all religions and no religions
belief desystem. In a book of exquisite
poems that shift perception and action,
there's a truth in the editor's undivision.

It is one example. I feel there are many
variations. Variables and denominators
of God. Realworld metaphors of light
and death. Melodies of birds. Colours

of earth that are ours and not. To embrace
the pantagogue that drives out bad light –
atmospheres with clogged filters.

Today, Tracy and I will breathe the best air
we can access and share. The grey
strike-thrush that's preter-nesting
is exemplary in its scrutiny
of a semi-fallen branch.
The complications of all our common ancestry,
our Oneness and open arms
to ward off the daily ruse de guerre
of the so-called rich and powerful.

JK

24.

There is in this a fantasy, and a kind of reprimand:
the chastening those who boast of emptying give to me.
They who lay their bodies out, their neat sinewy bodies
on rattan mats, and empty themselves
of all boundaries, all limits, of fences, all gates,
all walls, or structures, all those tiny cubicles
of meaning – the cloisters, the cloisters, the cloisters –
that fantasy is the fantasy of wide open fields.
It is something like how I imagine a river was named
"Snake" before they could see it from above as we do now;
how they had to find on the nearest mountain, a look-
out point over the stretch of Wyoming's earth,
to see the s-pattern of that meandering river,
a purple line on the green and tawny landscape,
and there call it "Snake", a warning of sin, yes, but
mostly an allusion to the brazen snake on a long pole held
up to heal the travellers dusty with adventure,
who still had water in their leather pouches, and enough
desire to keep going, even after leaving some
in Nebraska – those who said, "The Platte is enough
for us, and we will change our name to the people
who will plant trees along the road, where others
may stop before their push over the mountains."
There is a Gnosticism to that way of seeing:
no end to walking, no end to the sky, no end
to the living and the dead, and this is another
thing I admire, but do not share. I have made
my peace with the monkish cell, the blank walls,
the dank corners, the austere bed, the single
window looking out to the tiny universe of its
limits. I have settled on the prayer mat, the eyes
shut tight and the gamble of imagining – this may be
the last frontier for me, and I accept its laws,
the comforting limits that this body seems to need.

We have just returned after three thousand miles
stretching the limits of our world, moving
through the open frontier that once was impossibly
grand, but now is closed in by the confines
of the highway, the pocket of air in the cabin
of our car, the sound of athletes in Rio grunting
out their efforts, the wit of the British commentators,
the sense of being in a world at once broad
as our unknowing, and limited by what we know;
we arrive as one would from prayer, the prison
of faith. The world is a meditation on what little
I know, and what little I will know. I know why
I say, "love", why I say this is one way to expand
on the rituals of arrival and departure – I say, "love"
for it remains the only constant, perhaps, and even
then it is an act of faith to profess this.

KD

25.

At New Norcia, where the grain crops are heady
and the Moore River is flowing fast, the Benedictine
monk, Chris, comes over and introduces himself.

He says the sun shines and next week he will
perform with other monks skits out of Dante's
Inferno. He is a little concerned about the outcome

but looking forward to it nonetheless. I tell him
how once I was going to stay at the monastery
"in retreat" at the suggestion of Sister Veronica

Brady who was concerned that my then-alcoholism
was eating my life and spirit away. I am not of
the church, or of anything else these days,

not in that way. I take my spirit with me,
however I travel, and I feel it is intact and sorting
itself out with its contacts with day-to-day life –

it is a permeable membrane. He tells me of a twelve-step
group run in the monastery for the greater community,
and I laugh over how much another monk at lunch

earlier (they served us a wonderful vegan plateful)
offered wine and when politely turned down, settled
to quickly polish off the wine of his own labours.

It's not an easy place, a mission on Noongar land,
and all that was taken from the people whose land it is,
but the last Yued speaker is the old ex-Abbot

who spent years saturating himself in the knowledge.
I am trying to unravel it all now, and brother Chris
is there shaking my hand furiously, and saying,

"You bring light with poetry", and then seeing
Tracy, says, "I must greet the Carmelite postulant!"
though Tracy's time behind the great walls,

standing for meals, in her bare cell and wearing
coarse cloth, was thirty years ago. But for Chris,
however far she has gone from the order,

she is still part of what it is he has spent
his thirty-five years doing. He talks with Tracy
about a senior Carmelite sister they both know,

saying it's so rare for the Carmelites to leave
the convent, but she was recovering from illness
and the peace up here in the country aided her recovery.

Chris was reluctant, I think, to see us go, and I, strangely,
was reluctant to let go of the conversation. Ring-necked
parrots with hooked beaks that opened forbidden

and unforbidden fruit with clinical and obvious ease,
flew sharp and fast and close to us, and Dante's tools
with which he laid bare *Inferno* flew with them.

JK

26.

Hard to believe that just beyond these miles of bridges
across the wide delta's flooding of grandeur,
a chronicler with a penchant for the epic pronouncement,
a woman dressed in hand-woven garments that punish
the body, might write the terrible story of our world.
The almighty's arm arrives as a quick and sudden
hammer, the music of the green spaces set off into
a noise of lament. By the time we near Baton Rouge,
I think of how green it all seems, how fecund it tastes,
this thick air, while on the radio, a giddy woman
replays her recordings of bears and wolves, and meadow
larks, of percolating bogs and brooks, saying,
"We must keep these, these amazing sounds
because we may be archiving our future" – which in her
voice does not have the weight of doom, just this
giddy sense of how "cool", how "awesome" it is
to hear the brush of the grizzly's fur against the mic.
And were I the prophet, I think I would begin
by complaining that my eyes have been seared to an
opaque miasma, stunned by the constant sun off the highway
I cannot see, and when I say this, the voice (there is
always a voice) tells me I have been blessed with blindness.
You know the cliché of the thing; it is what all who
must see must understand, that before the catastrophes
of chaos, there will be the purity of blindness, a preparation
for the deepest sorrows. I promise that I will learn
the language of these last days, and the songs that we
must sing to find a path to a new day, and if it all seems
like a cultish indulgence, forgive me, but I live among
those who have mastered the language of denial,
and that, too, has a long history. I have imagined
this place of green space, jewelled with the red

roofs of houses, the gleaming silver of rusting zinc sheets,
the startling opal of houses painted by a people
who know that bright colours cause demons to tremble
and flee, as an open morose sea – and this too strikes me
as a prophet's vision. It is a start. It is easy to forget
these things in the heart of the city, with its narrow
lanes and bodies moving as if the world's daily
tribulations are enough for now. The air is heavy
with the oils of every green thing there is, and my son
laughs, "My skin will be beautiful when I am done
here." And he is right. We will leave him to it,
and there will be a gap, the emptiness of separation,
but that is why we pray. In the mean time, what must
a prophet do? Eat, pay the bills, sleep for hours
and hope for the holiness to remain his constant;
that dreams may come with the language he needs
to speak into this world. For weeks I worried about
the monstrosity of Trump, as if he is the end of days;
now, I know that he too will be swept by the storms,
and this may be the first song of lamentation.

KD

27.

Here, Kwame, the prophets are suppressed
by gunfire and crop-dusters, by the rise of the right
to lawmakers, by the filling in of wetlands and blasting
of entire red mountain ranges. It's by the sports team
not winning enough medals, by the abyss
widening between a nation's love of travel
and its rejection of those travelling towards its shores
for a stay beyond their holiday savings. We travel (traverse?)
the dangerous road to the city today, a weather front
coming in; we travel so Tim can do his Goethe
Society class. Tracy and I will wait in the car
at Reabold Hill, in the 430 hectare Bold Park bush
reserve on the coast, and watch the white-cheeked
honeyeaters watching the sheet of the front
come in across shipping lanes. The windows
of the car will grow steamy and the anomaly
of bush in the middle of the city will emphasise
through the separation from the revelatory
acts of wind and rain impacting the tuart trees,
the sentinel banksias showing signs of dieback,
and the thought that my mother said last week,
that park, that hill – highest point on the coastal
plain – "…is in some way associated with your
Dad's side of the family". She recalls this from
across forty-six years when they divorced.
She holds no grudges. She never claims
even the slightest vestige of prophecy,
though prides herself on good sense.
She left all religions, though still
remains entranced by the gnostics.
Our parents, Kwame, and our sons.
And their learning. And our separate lives.

JK

28.

for Joe Higgs (1940-1999)

Joe Higgs, a voice that long caught the sweet
pain of the minor (Kingston, circa 1965),
humbles me this morning with this lyric
of tender defiance: "Everyday my heart is
sore/ Seeing that I am so poor…" – something
recorded in the bubbly sluggishness of early
ska, with the masterful reggae stop-time genius
of vocal phrasing, Delroy Wilson – sufferahs
in dusty sandals who were poor, and still
in that instant of despair could sing
with rugged harmony, "'Cause there's
a reward for me". O reggae, how you render
redundant this stammering tongue, how you
take this gloom-dark morning, and turn
Sancho Panza's quarrelling at the absurd
antics of his master from La Mancha, mouth
empty of molars, resumé festooned with
absurd defeats, into something as righteous
as a dread dallying through Kingston on
a S90. We know that time can collapse
when the soul reaches for its music and finds
it in the soft part of early morning when
the light is cloud-filtered – and here I am
in Nebraska singing Kingston, Spain, Australia,
Cuba, Eritrea, Mexico, the music of darkness and light,
and what more can I offer than what I call
melancholy, the hunger for more and more
love – how I imagine the reward for me:

Though I am burdened down with shame
There's no one for me to blame,
But I shall not give up so easy, no
'Cause there's a reward for me…

Play it, John, and maybe deep in there,
when you arrive at the end of words,
you will find me waiting for you,
to skank through the morning,
two grown men in their loose garments
caught up in the breeze, with their healing
wounds and limping gaits, singing
full-voiced and hopeful as angels:

There's a reward for me
There's a reward for me

KD

29.

Music underwrites, Kwame. No, too fiscal –
it interfaces and links the words that accrue
across the day. Mid-air, inside my head,
I am thinking of the relationship between
typos and music. In a book of twenty years
writing, a book of writing on handwriting,
I just found an "introduced" typo. Not in my
original, but I should have picked it up
in proofs. Orthographical arpeggios.
Anyway, this typo consisted of the insertion
of a letter "d" after a capital "F" – an easy
mistake given f & d are side by side
on the qwerty keyboard. And where
I had "Fur" it now says, bolded, "Fdur",
which, interestingly, is German for F major.
Music is mentioned (hip-hop) in the poem,
though I'd be working the etymologies
hard to unearth the German connection.
I've no doubt it's there. As I've no doubt
that in accommodating the failure of setting,
the letters leaping back up from the mess
of the hellbox, I've signalled my inability
to escape music even when there's no sound
other than a humming fluorescent tube
and the sound of my fingers on the keys
striking fast and with a reasonable
degree of accuracy.

JK

30.

These days I have started writing in white ink
on black stretches of paper – there is something
precarious about the thick flow of white lines
against the black, something, I suppose, that makes
each letter seem indelible, as if now I cannot make
an error. I remember the hours I would spend
making dots, thousands and thousands of them,
with the superstition of someone driven by
obsession, or like a walk racer, holding the body back
from its impulse to run, yet hurtling forward,
leaning the body forward to make speed
with terrible and painful restraint. It is like
that, this bright whiteness opening like a conjuror's
trick across the page. I am starting to gather
metaphors for our art, John, stories that I want
to share with the new makers of poems who need
the distraction of humility and insignificance
that comes with the fixation on craft, the making
of things, to free them of self-importance – the curse we
all wear at least for a time. This is easy,
as it happens: the sushi master; the seamstress,
her mouth full of pins; the deejay spinning;
the basket weaver; the dizzying dancer spinning
and falling, and spinning and falling; the drummer
repeating a roll and repeating a roll and repeating –
the cycle of mistakes built on mistakes, built on mistakes.
My lines are not words, they are characters
finding their symmetry across this black open
space, and if I step back, what I see is light
seeping in through the walls of my hovel;
and this is enough. I vowed to allow myself
only one such lyric each month, and this is it:
This art is the making of light on an intact dark page.

KD

31 .

To whom we address. I say unto. Dear X.
I speak for myself. In praise of. With gratitude.
A creator? À la Gerard Manley Hopkins, over-
stuffing lines with the intensity of encounter.
In the face of. By comparison. I am. Diminutive.
All of this. How dare I. Glory and credit due.
But infallible? In the remeasuring of where we live
on this block, I follow swarms back to their
respective hives. I sound out. Reposition.
Take notice. Apostrophise at a semi-safe
distance from the yawning mouths in hollowed
trees that during some storm or other will split,
spill their etymologies. Insect words. Evidence
of such falling is everywhere, strewn across
the acres. These patterns of interior selves
we build out of the debris of "perfection".

JK

32.

The roads and stretches of open fields
of Dorchester County carry the hush
of a battlefield after the victors have
slouched on to new fronts, and the bodies
of their dead are buried in shallow graves.
There is history and there is now.
The dead are strewn over every surface –
golden as if giant gingkos have shed –
bees, first drunk with the spray
of pesticides and then the burning,
and then the deaths. I have been
looking for language to soften this,
but it is carnage, the terrible dismantling
of the order of things. For us,
the hand of nature or God is easier,
as all helplessness is rescued
by the reassurances of fatalism,
but someone ordered the planes
to fly low through the county,
and cough out clouds of Naled
to consume the mosquitoes,
to halt the panic of Zika;
and the officials speak with the calm
sombreness of generals – collateral,
they say, it is what happens.
At dawn, the heat in the hives
was too much here in the deep
southern land, and the bees gathered,
a beard of companionship
against the outer-hives, humming
cool air into their bodies,
when the planes came.

KD

33.

The distance between a Facebook page
and a mineshaft where vigilantes threaten

to drop the murdered is so very small.
Behind screens is only part of the damage,

it's when bigots emerge from self-
illumination, self-images in their eyes,

that it all comes together: the running down,
the killing, the justifications. In the mining towns

the burrowing down to what might be at the core
of belief is also an attempt at erasure: to mine

away souls. But desecrators unearth
their own demons, digging deep to find

the white goods they desire: as Dr Plot
conjectured in 1667: "lapides sui generis,

naturally produced by some extraordinary
plastic virtue, latent in the earth..." this fossil

record we turn ourselves inside out for,
reaching too low. And so, frontiers

are made on the field of the screen,
and Kalgoorlie – out there – epicentre

of the goldfields, cutting edge of race riots,
Superpit-proud of the venal seams in the Aussie flag,

flexes its Midas touch on God's Own Country
while a dead boy's family grieve and grieve and grieve.

JK

34.

for John Kinsella

On the road, you long for the like-minded,
those who will not argue when you take bread
and share it with the hungry; those who will
nod and add their cup of wine to the gift,
and whisper that indeed around the bend,
just further down river, there is a town
where all the things given can be replenished.
At night, you sleep well with companions
of the road like this. None would call it
courage, but that is the language I know –
men and women who laugh at adversity
and say, "Ahh, we walk the way of Old Campaigners!"
They are the courageous ones, for they
grant you courage and peaceful sleep.
In search of a metaphor on a cool autumn
afternoon, during that quiet space where
the news has settled as a gloom over things,
but the mind has space to daydream, I arrived
at the fantasy of the shelter of the comrade-in-arms,
the tailor's shop, the one who has come to know
each curve and lump of your body, all
the errors of eating and starving, the wounds
of abuse inflicted by enemies, by friends and
by our own hands. They know the shape
of an ankle, the way it limps; they have measured
the length of the inner thigh to the crotch,
the swell of the shoulders, and the folds
of the neck-back; they know where your body
desires comfort and embrace and where it longs
for the cushion of air; they can tell how you feel
flattered by the contours of fabric chosen right,
and they have studied you so well, that you

have asked if they will dress you when you
are laid out for good – not so much the tailor,
the named one, but the thing that he does,
the sensation of a shirt of river-washed cotton
slipping over your body like water, the magical
ease of it on the skin, as if made like a second
skin, like the embrace of a lover that never
grows heavy or awkward – that is the metaphor
for the companion on the road I cherish.
For what is certain is that the road will be rough,
and the wounds will continue, and the betrayers
will abound, and the sorrow will be certain;
but the like-minded ones, those that fit you
well, those are the ones I have come to hold
dear, the ones that share the burdens of this art
of feeling all torment, so as to bear true witness.

KD

35.

Thanks for the dedication, Kwame.
I get it. I get the road and travelling
companions who are there like shadow.

Today, I have been among the spring birds:
rufous whistlers, trillers, red-capped robins,
grey shrike-thrushes, 28 parrots, thornbills.

They have formed no analogies with human
activities, and I have just watched and listened
and filled in the spaces between twig and leaf

with their sensory intensities. This isn't projection
as it's nesting time and that's as intense as it gets.
A grey-shrike thrush searching for insects

on the same branch as a brown honeyeater
singing hard at it. Warning? Carnivore
to nectarvore? A conversation of proximity

that fills the eroded spaces in my neural network.
And I wonder how fast I change in the process
of absorption: the winding down of the body,

the background radiation changing the narrative
in little and large ways – it's eighteen becquerels
per cubic metre here because of all the granite,

but that's so much less than the cities of the Northern
hemisphere. Granites pushing always upwards,
their skins flaking, lit up with their own ancient

history, watching their shadows grow as soil erodes
away around them, then diminishing as they themselves
defoliate in rough open air. A commitment to being,

then going. Static, almost, and on the road, almost.
Companions to each other, though bulldozers blade
them out lopsided when the machines can manage

enough leverage. So, here I am as evening closes in
and daybirds hand over recitation duties to nightbirds: owls
and frogmouths. And, on the cusp, I look to open

nest-space in my head where I have remembered
before but have lost a smidgen of what happened,
of what I so wanted to remember in passing.

JK

36.

I keep rehearsing the body's shifting of gear,
although it would be a lie to pretend
I ever felt so robust in my body as to ignore
decay – the thorn in the ankle, its constant
aching even at rest; the ready limp
at some sudden misstep; the years of my
stomach's wreck – how odd that with age
some strange chemistry has eased that portend
of a quite painful death. Still, making poems,
I have determined, will become the same
as the search for language – not the language
I call mine, but a foreign one. I speak
Spanish like a man playing charades – there
is something improvisational about the desperate
quest for ways around the absence of words,
how when I must say a wall, and I have
no bank of it in my head, I begin to piece
together a grand metaphor of familiar
words to offer clues of meaning to the one
who stands and listens with that amused
fascination that audiences have when I read
a poem – the command is in the reaching
for something that is not there. But with
Spanish, it is really not there, was never there,
but more and more, with poems, it seems
something was there, and I can't reach it,
so I invent the wall, the shape of it, the use
of it, the weight of it, the meaning of it,
when I can't find the word to say wall;
and this, wonderfully, is called art.
Failure, of course. I am reading DeLillo
these days, slouching through the myth
of genius, and finding myself arriving
at this same place of empathy – you know,

the way you can tell that a moment he tries
to replicate is, deep inside him, far more
beautiful than he has found the language for;
in this case, that "Giants win the pennant!"
moment reads flat as history. Oh well,
this is how we fail – or age with nobility, yes?

KD

37.

I don't know what to do with age or time
or the temporal in any configuration
at the moment... the moment!... Kwame.
I feel lost in the matrix, the vortex, and this
without any pop-cultural allusions outside
knowing such allusions exist, that what I write
might be read in such contexts. No,
in this country where the far right
are flaunting their racism, where debates
over what is and isn't racist draw the chatter
of Facebookers and Twitterers and Instagrammers
away from the horror in their own backyards,
I forget I am middle-aged or old or young
or just that proverbial association of atoms
doing what the rest of the universe
is doing. I heard today that some fashion
designer, who has the sensitivity
that goes with the exploitation of body
and the worship of the market as art,
used designer dreadlocks in his show
and it was met by social media outcry
because his use was a sign of cultural
appropriation. Now, in his case with his
pristine white models (and non-whites? I don't
know), it might well be the case, but as someone
who had dreadlocks for many years
I can assure all the horrified that I had
no intentions, outside having very long curly
hair that was politically and ethically
left unkempt. My hair naturally dreadlocks.
I haven't combed my hair in thirty-five
years and have no intention of ever
doing so, but I wear it short because
long hair irritates me and having to part

my dreadlocks at night to balance my head
sent me nuts, and the fact of another arrest
and a notoriously unsympathetic judge
meant it better to lop them off
in order to stay out of the cells
long-term. That's the matter-of-fact
of it. Nothing to do with "style". I am
without style, or at least am indifferent
to it. Why do you wear only black then?
I am asked. Why not? I don't have to think
about style. Style is a capitalist trick.
I am not playing. And identity is consumed
by the i-Phone, by the computer, by the market
place laughing all the way to the stock-exchange
and their faceless shareholders. That's
where it's happening, this unpicking
of respect and justice, of fairness
and equality. I sit here worrying
because my brother's stepdaughters
have just arrived in Australia wearing
their full head-coverings, proud of their
Muslim heritages, and absolutely decent
in their respect for difference. I worry
as my shearer brother – fairest man
I have ever known – takes
them out to the bush,
out where the votes
swelled for the anti-Muslim
anti-anything but Euro-whites
and racist incidents are commonplace.
I wonder how many of these bigots
have Celtic ancestry, as much evidence
shows the Celtic warriors were likely
dreadlocked fundamentalists. In their ways.
And they were far from peaceful, shall we say.
Stephen's stepdaughters are cool,

calm and collected. They are reasonable
people. They have a Facebook friendship
with Stephen's own daughter. They
use gadgets just like the bigots.
They don't impose their faith
on anyone. Live and let live.
Hopefully they'll go through
their holiday without a problem.
But I worry, because it's headlines
every day. The bigots have mobilised.
My mother, who speaks Malay, has welcomed
the girls with a cake saying, "Selamat datang".
I send them the same greeting.
I admired Bob Marley
and he had the best dreads.
But I didn't have dreadlocks
because I was stealing from Bob.
My hair dreadlocks and I shared few
manners with where I came from.
It wasn't a style. It wasn't even religious.
But it was spiritual, sort of.
Brothers. Sisters. All of us ageless.

JK

38.

I have returned to a life of numbers;
this is the law that panic creates in me.
Of course, the panic fades since death,
slow and messy, is the terror that I first
imagined, then the days continue and it is
clear that long before that there will be
joys and strange happenings, or not...
The rest... well you know the rest. Still,
there are greater terrors, and now that
those I meet each day mutter about
how it wouldn't be so bad to have a tyrant
as a leader, it occurs to me that that terror,
at least, has not left me. It may have to do with
that pompous sneer, the bully's curled lip,
the bobbing head, and the greatest shame
of facing tyranny and knowing full well
that one can only win with macabre jokes
and a clown's disposition. This cannot be
enough, but it is all we have now, I fear.
So I count the numbers, carbs, proteins,
sugar, steps – each day a calculus of my
blood's betrayal. I promise myself only
a handful of indulgences on this theme;
after all, it has been done before, and far
better, when the news is grimmer, and who
should sanction redundancy? That should
not be encouraged. Let us speak of righteous
things, for a change. Like this, from the ever
melodious Morgan Heritage: "Yuh don't have
to dread to be Rasta", which is a front way
of saying that old truth that we wear
our crowns with the hope that they may
announce the heartical truths we carry,
and the holy dread was a holy dread

long before the tyranny of style. "You
don't have to be rasta to be dread,"
must be true, too, in the annals of this world.

KD

39.

So often the machine in the flower,
the machine in the painting, the poem.
Those short sharp clauses; realisations.
But that's not the answer for me. Or for?
Lyrical bent of the juvenile, black-headed
monitor out in a slow spring, a cedilla
on the eucalypt, lost in the bark, parsing
the crusader beetle. Imagine the history
we could labour this with, forgetting
other histories happening slant.
I listen to Django Reinhardt's jaunty
guitar but deny the machine – plenty
of weed flowers outside the window
but we can't smell any. I think. As I suffer
from hay fever different registers come into play.
    Different non-machinic calibrations.

JK

40.

for Tuhin Das

He wakes to the crowding of birds,
he does not know their names, he has
never looked to see their colours –
as if to see them gathered by his window
would be to let them invade. They know
he is inside, they are waiting each dawn
for him to look. He listens, a cup of coffee
in his hands, until, like a mob dispersing,
the noises begin to fade, and then one
protester remains – a cry of alarm.
His hosts ask him if he likes the sound
of the birds. They imagine that these
gentle mornings in another country,
where the air is cool early, and the sound
of neighbours slipping through the narrow
lanes, carrying only ordinary cares –
what bills to pay, what the father's
hospice care will cost, where to drink
tonight – are a healing for him, and there
in the city, birds, crowds of them
spinning in the cooler air, would seem
so alien, they will be a comfort.
He says he hears the birds – they are
startling – it is the word he uses
with the hope that they will not see
his alarm. He will never tell them
they are haunting him, following him
across the seas, over the land, waiting
to circle him and devour him – that is
his nightmare. The poet lives in exile;
this is his identity. But this is not who
he is. He is the tamer of trees,

the one who has learned an alien skill,
how to tame a boisterous tree, with pruning
and care, into something like a toy, a breathing
creature, small as a man's arm, the compaction
of detail, every leaf counted, every tiny
stunted limb a sinewy thing. Against
the scrim of canvas over his window,
the tree is a brief, pithy soliloquy,
like that wizened actor shuffling across
the stage, then standing in the twilight
pooling about him and saying to the world:
"They chased me deep into the night,
I changed my houses each night, and I grew
silent, keeping every dream I have had,
and every vision given to me, deep inside
me, so that they will not hear me, those
wild birds, who will follow me as far
as a man can go. Now, I am old, and dying,
and so I will step out into the light
and speak to you, tell you how to be kind
to each other, and this small secret,
that even freedom is its own prison."
You might think that to say this
is a dream would be to defang it of its
terror, or turn it into a manageable
surrealism, but for the poet, his dreams
are the deepest truths. He wakes up
with the voice of his friends crying,
while their killers grunt with each
blunt blow of the knives, the whisper
of blood, the terrible sound of a man
saying, "Mama, Mama, they are killing me."

KD

84

41.

The web existed long before "technology" –
what allows me to tell you that yesterday
I wrote a poem for my son on surrealism
and birds and his absence. That now,
as everyday, I write looking through my
window at birds looking in, that it is the core
image of my parley with the world. That
this moment a "28" parrot that shouldn't – we are told –
even be here is flexing its yellow chest over
a sea of capeweed flowers, a yellow underlay.
Or that every morning our son Tim rises
and through his window watches the birds
with the dawn, watches the nests being
tended, watches and records all in his bird book,
and then turns his interactions into fine poems.
That he knows every name and speaks
with the birds. But there's more, too,
as Bangladesh is a pivotal place
in the configuration of my youth,
and some of my early poems attempt to reach
into its complexities, its beauties, its traumas.
Tim asks me about Dhaka often, as the world
is fascinating and intense and exquisite to him,
and he plans his own journeys, watching
birds he knows the name of, that are free
and active and building outside his consciousness.
These webs woven forever, these webs
birds sew their nests together with,
these webs that carry far more than
fibre-optic cable, than the entire
electromagnetic spectrum.

JK

42.

for Sancho Panza

My sisters told me they thought the servant
a clown – "squire" I think was the translation –
but I can't remember why. That was thirty
years ago, perhaps more. But they would
rehearse the complaints he made at being
beaten, and the way he stripped the delusional
knight of his dignity while still keeping
a shred of grace in all that he did. This was
a strange kind of beauty – they spoke it with
laughter. Now I understand the genius
of Cervantes, and find comfort in the sinful
ways of Sancho Panza, how entirely
holy he seems in his flawed indulgence,
in his self-serving heroism, in the pure
comic power of his gentle cajoling of the Don,
illustrious fool. I am walking with them
these days, navigating my neighbourhood
of fall dryness, every other house with its
roof colonised by roofers laying tiles,
as if there has been a boom in cut-rate
supplies, but it was just this one hailstorm,
and the roofers are making a killing. It is,
though, the story of Cardenio and Lucinda
that, with roof-litter, marks each mile of this walk,
each house, each spot, a kind of dying
of my world in the mood of lament, regret,
violence and lurid melodrama, and so
this flat, bland city, Lincoln, has assumed
the shape and texture of stony foothills
where a heartbroken man tortures
himself by not killing himself, his mind
rehearsing the betrayal of love – all quite

lurid. It is how I push back against
the noise of blood and the looming
prospect of a diabolic comic sneering
his path into power. These are brief
sabbaticals, as satisfying as a mindless
soap, but somehow full of the edification
of brilliant language – the stuff that outlasts
the reign of kings, tyrants, emperors,
the rise and fall of empires, hegemonies,
and monstrosities. Each day, as the air
cools, and the world turns into an orange
wash, light softening as it always does,
there is a brief respite, and then
I return to time, its ordinary enslavement,
the body's decay, the counting of coins,
the annoyances, the laughter, the art
of making poems, and this, too, is good;
the kind of thing a good squire must embrace,
bruised, bewildered, and still able to stand.

KD

43.

I find it difficult to lift the sun from the east,
to set it in the horizon, the holy grail paddocks
that yield cockeyed seed and blood.

I find it difficult to read lines that hide their ends,
running downhill, eroding with heat and flood,
while denying their roots in chant.

I find it difficult to tune out the percussion
of detonators, the rapidity of gunpowder
cajoling the projectile to its bitter end.

I find it difficult to raise the dead from texts
in flashy new covers, old stories repackaged
to make them alive for a volatile market.

I find it difficult to accept that anaesthesia
excising a few hours from my life
relieves me of pain.

I find it difficult apportioning more time
to praise all living things than to condemning
the annihilation of all living things.

I find it difficult setting the sun in the west,
balancing it on the dark thread of its glow,
orange heart begging to remain.

JK

44.

It is as if we were not expecting it,
and perhaps we were not, not now,
anyway, but the mornings are darker,
a kind of heavy smoky dark, and we
move through the city with headlamps,
as if we are heading for some secret
place, a place where people will gather
in a circle, half asleep yet expectant
and proud of having made it through
the empty streets to this place, the few,
chosen for this alone, to rehearse
what we know, what we have known,
and to lament what we do not know.
But the darkness makes us guarded,
people who know that silence can be
useful. Here is how we argue these
days, two people who have been in
the same room for decades, we wait
for the tripwires, and then, with
grace and ease, we step over them,
and allow the long pause to suck
all heat from the air. When we speak
again the air is lighter, and a war
has been fought and lost without
a drop of blood being shed. So many
people in this world, in this country
are like us, like the people gathered
in the room who are drinking
thin coffee. They stay the hour
before stepping out into the light
of the morning and remark how
quickly the sun rises. I get the sense
that if one were to manage this
all winter, you would survive it –

barely, it is true, but survival
nonetheless. And perhaps this is all
we have – the skill to carry our
balmlike silence, the thing that mutes
all pain, with us always, and the art
to know how to use it mercifully.

KD

45.

Another environmental outrage here, Kwame.
A neighbouring shire has manipulated a boundary

and cleared old-growth trees from the edge
of a nature reserve. I had been going into campaign

mode to try and stop them. We went out to visit
these old wandoos and salmon gums – vital

nesting trees, as it takes over a century of growth
and work by fire and termites, fungi and storms,

by all the natural acts of existence, for suitable
hollows to form on limbs and trunks, places

where cockatoos and parrots can lay eggs,
rear their chicks. Fewer and fewer of such

trees are left, as the land is ravaged by farmers
and developers and miners greedy for every

foothold. We must ensure that on the edges
and in the niches, these habitats persist.

But to go out and see the massacre
unleashed – the horror of butchered

tree corpses, and a lone pink and grey
galah looking on from a remaining

nesting hollow in a nearby tree:
it imprints deep. Even the sunset

is bereft. But I've no room for metaphor –
it feels tainted, it feels like insult to injury, to death.

JK

46.

It is not as if my head is empty of words;
hardly, there is much chaos there,

and the twisted scowl of that demagogue,
the one so easy to declare a dangerous

monstrosity, the one who leaves us dumbfounded,
filled with a sense of absurd wordlessness,

for how can one find language for the most
obvious things? And is this the time for us

to ask the nature of evil, the nature of fools,
the way of buffoons, the acts of bigots?

One seasoned monarch copied down the wisdom
of his sages – old people who formed

the language to contain the better things we do –
asked us never to answer a fool in his foolishness,

then, just as quickly, admonished us to always
speak to a fool to correct him, and it is true

that one is tempted to choose one or the other –
though buried in this conundrum is an older

truth, that a fool is rarely as foolish as he seems,
and all foolishness is an act of counter-wisdom,

which is, in itself, a way of knowing, and the crude
acts we carry out come from a way of knowing

that has drawn a swathe of destruction over the earth.
So I have stopped calling a fool a fool, at least

this fool, for he is more than that, he is older
than that, he is the one who makes the prophet say,

"Who needs a prophet when the people choose
to be blind?" I understand the story of destruction,

at least how it is tied to the way of true want, the hunger
for accumulating – those who in a year turned a simple

trade in furs into a slaughter of millions – all that blood,
all that flesh, all that coin collected, all those fortunes

made. I know how the discovery of veins of lead can turn,
in a decade, into a carnival of the enslaved, the poisoning

of the blood of black people, a deficit from one generation
to the next as they mine the lead to make the bullets

that rule them, that contain them; and the land is left
bereft of the memory of its meaning and beauty. It is

a matter of scale. I understand this now, and this is another
of those petrifying truths: where must we go, and what

must we do with all this knowing? Which is why I say
to the complaining poets, do not begrudge the troubadour

with his raspy voice and jangling guitar, who let his body
fall into the trance of all trances, to conjure from his

silence these long lamentations of wisdom that settle
on us, and drag us from that deepest silence. We all

begin to sing before we know what we are singing,
and if we are lucky, what we are singing is healing truth.

KD

47.

In being out of contact, Kwame, I have been in contact
with what might be made, what might eventuate. But also

prospects of loss. On the edge of the Nullarbor Plain, Tim
and I heard the rustling song of the almost vanished Nullarbor

quail thrush. Tim identified it out of the sunset by matching it
with a description he'd read. The soundings of text. And later,

seven hundred or so kilometres further on in Ceduna, he confirmed
the "sighting", listening to a recording made by an old birdman

decades ago, uploaded into modernity. That moment together,
that light caught in the bluebush to mark our way. A living

memorial? I find the thought of such loss too grievous to write
out fully. We are witnessing ourselves out of these pictures. Out

where no photograph will take, out where no old negative
or new digitalisation will take, will collect all the evidence

of presence, its layers of deceit, the grand conceit
of perspective. The song was plaintive but playful.

JK.

48.

The mornings have darkened, the roads have suddenly
grown unfamiliar – I missed a turn, improvised a path
back to the gloomy familiar, and the lights darting

through the cold ashen air quickened my heart. It happens
each year, and still I feel as if the things I don't know
are slipping away from me. In the darkness, though,

I remember you and Tim, the tenderness of listening
to the open world, picking out the bird song, drip
by drip, how much like prayer this must be – a body

straining at first to hear the voice of God saying
turn left, or turn right, or return, or go forward.
How the world's cacophony overwhelms even

the most holy of us, until we grow still, until we
can pick out the wheat from the dross, until the voice
arrives. No, I have to admit I have not waited long

enough to hear the bird song in this land, and this
is how I feel about so much that is precious in this world,
so much that is going away from us. What I mean is

I feel as if I cannot stay long enough to be consumed
by a single thing, so deeply, so thoroughly that even
for an instant, I can imagine I know all there is to

know of it. I am browsing through my old journals,
browsing through, I mean, my imagined life with what
I feel is a kind of familiar shame at how little I have

retained, how much I have invented my own history
as a compensation for my failings, for what I did not
know then. There is a small comfort here, and a lesson

that we do change by increments of correction, and
it is possible to envy and pity that younger self who
was searching for tomorrow. It has been thirty years –

I can say this – that I have kept from my pages
the name of Tony Bird, a squawking African white
man, weaving poems of loss and lament, a melancholy

I found in him that made me write
in the deep Canadian winter, January
1987: *Passport is still missing. I am listening*

to this song by the guy Tony Bird, "Nothing But Time".
I love it. It's so powerful as a visual poem
and a very nostalgic sound hovers through it.

The memory of a dead, green-eyed, red-haired girl.
Excellent. I search for this bird song online, no luck.
He is scattered here and there on the web, sort

of a splintered sound, not quite coming back
together, perhaps like memory. But I realise
I remember the words, and I remember learning

the song, and how while singing it, I would
darken her eyes and her hair, a way to make
a home of this and the Zambezi and the Africa

in his art, in his voice, in my own making.
All of this to say, John, that I envy the hearing,
the way in which you can mourn what we are

losing because you are there at the portal
to see it slip away, while the rest of us wake
one morning, and feel this heavy weight

of loss and mourning, not knowing what we
have lost, but knowing only that we have.

KD

49.

Last night, I spoke in Sydney about keeping
an activist poetry journal – I have kept one for
thirty years now. Another strange synchronicity

that makes this exchange of poems more than
a collation or collecting of poetic interludes. *It makes*.
How we make poems from our witnessings. While walking

with Tracy and Tim and our friend and host Peter Minter,
we passed under a tree foliated with flying foxes bristling
towards the twilight. They rose up and spread their

Halloween wings to chart the skyscraper skies,
to test the limits of range and knowledge, to quote
their own conscious indifference to the consumer fad

of a night that is not short or thin here, but widening
with the approach of summer. The shops are full of goods
to make a Halloween "local", to segue flying foxes

with Hollywood and television, to make a net
of things they might latch onto, sucking the fruit
of its goodness, the substance of reality.

JK

50.

November 3, 2016

I am, these days, mapping out the road ahead,
the way I plan a drive at dusk, choosing in my
head the paths I know best, where the lights
are always lit, and the eyelets in the streets
sparkle as guides for me. There will always
be terrors, but I have discovered a small joy
in driving alone – what I do not see, what I almost
destroy but avoid through the grace of angels,
cannot frighten blissful me. Instead, I am a ship
on a dark ocean, imagining only the universe
of monsters just beneath my hull; the sweet
deep sleep of darkness comforts me. Of course,
it is easy to tell, perhaps, that these are the days
before the news arrives of who will lead
this country; at least so it seems, but the news
I am waiting for is the millions who will wake the day
after the count, filled with the righteous
satisfaction of having seen a restoration
of the proper order of things. It is they
I fear most and am wary of. You see, I, too,
have walked through these eight years
as if walking inside a miracle that has
its clear expiration date. We have done
nothing to deserve this, and soon it too,
like all products of faith, will be taken away,
so that what is left is the profit of it all,
the capacity to believe in impossible things.
This is black humour. It will be a relief
if Trump wins, it will be the end of all
passive anger, it will be the end of all
pent-up resentments, it will be time again
for the sufferah to bear his sufferation

101

proudly with a well-trained screwface;
it will strip away the delusion of our
post-human mythos. When you shoot us
we will bleed. This is black humour:
no more dancing around the cry against
the man, the powers that be – how easy
a clean and bloody struggle is on the brain.
I am making a joke, of course, but I
must laugh in the face of what I fear.
When scowling bullies and liars win,
gloat, turn away from even the most
substantial complaint because they can,
I can either make black jokes of it all,
or I can squat in the corner and seethe.
I choose jokes. Next week, I will walk
without the soft language of Ferrante's novels
in my head, and I will listen to the birds,
as a kind of prayer, the way prayers
attach themselves to one another,
a chain link that takes us as far back
as our long history of bewilderment
at the cycles of the universe we see takes
us – the beginning of things, always
at the beginning of things, and this too
will be yet another lovely black joke.

KD

51.

The sickness is global. The greed is played out
in a grotesque theatre of manners and disturbance.
Out on the Hay Plain, said to be one of the flattest
places on the planet, the flat earth comes
into its own. I was asked at a recent event
how I respond to the "flat earthers"
regarding climate change, and now
I have found a metaphor that encompasses
the new order's endgame. It's a typically
Australian outback marker, a twisted memorial
to superiority and conquest, to a colonialism
of perceived emptiness, an "up yours" of vastness.
Along the side of the Sturt Highway in the middle
of the day, a kangaroo is poised to leap
out onto the road, in front of cars or trucks.
This is unusual – roos tend to leap across
roads at dusk or dawn, through the night,
sleeping and resting through the day.
To cross over to grazing grounds. Back.
But there he was, a large "red" boomer,
so we slowed rapidly. The boomer
reached for us, but halted mid spring,
until close enough we realised it was dead,
beholden to rigor mortis and empty eyed.
It has been propped into that position
by an 'Aussie' wit, no doubt. It's a typical
bush thing to do. Make of death a joke,
and to instil apprehension and horror
at once. Hit a roo and you can be wiped out.
A double entendre. I won't elaborate.
No need to decorate. We drove
on through saltbush, the roo
frozen in the windscreen,
the day heating up.

JK

52.

All morning there is an itch in my right hand,
on the second finger; it is flaming,
and I scratch this itch – a strange neurosis
in the gesture. I feel in a circle of errors;
the words I say return to me as stones,
and I am gradually growing silent. The pain
is not knowing whether the itch will stop –
which is like the pain of not knowing
if tomorrow will be better. Remember the way
we would sit in a happy courtyard of soft
sunlight on a cool day, and think how silly
sadness is, how comic fear is, how absurd
regret and conflict are. Nobody says these
things, but perhaps that is the way of happiness –
a failure of the imagination, or a failure
of memory, which is the same thing.
The clock on campus has been making
music all morning – it seems nonstop – as if
someone has forgotten to programme it right –
but no one else seems to notice, everyone
going about their business like characters
in a novel, full of witty banter and
the most banal of tales. How easily
they speak! I see no stones hurtling
through the room. I stare out
into the sky and think that I can
remember everything, I can write down
everything – which makes me the wounded
prophet of these dark days. I purpose to not
look outside my tiny cosmos, fearful
of the madness of carrying too much
in the head, of seeing the things I have
no answers for. I am in a room of light;
the desk is white, the glass is clean,

the noisy clock tower is a gleaming grey
in the dull dawn light, and my finger
is now red, flaming red and burning.

KD

53.

As the myriad birds fly towards the solar tower,
over the hectares of mirrors focusing the sun
on the eye of the tower — in synch, slightly out of kilter,
sequencing, staggered — flaming arcs to the ground,
they erupt in flame. The glare is an inferno.

In some zones of energy, they call this act
of incineration "ribbons". In one Californian
array, it happens every two minutes. The stench
of burning feathers, flesh, beaks and claws.
Where "alternative" fits with this we can't be sure,

but to concentrate the sun, to make the candles
burn beyond the warning of a lighthouse — a euphemistic
light that lures and blinds, a siren of searing vision
makes of us blind prophets. The tomatoes grown
by the supermarket chain as 'ecologically sound' —

all energy harnessed from this "new" technology —
ease the conscience at dinner tables not caught in the tower's
field of influence; no lashings of rope enough to hold
us to our perpetual masts, our axis of journeying.
Driving towards Port Augusta we fell victim,

not knowing what it was, this false beacon, this earth-
bound sun. And the salt-drenched Spencer's Gulf growing
more saline as the brine from the desalination plant
powered by the tower is pumped past bewildered mangroves,
cuttlefishes eggs tapering off into the whitening void.

The cult of the sun, its power over our every move,
our anxieties and moral greed — enough to provoke
the sacrifice of all living things and indifference to the dead.

JK

106

54.

"We know his heart of hearts,
and in his heart of hearts
he is a good man. A flawed
man, as all men are, but in his
heart of hearts, he is a good
man, and though he says things
that may hurt, he does not mean
to, for we know his heart of hearts,
and in his heart of hearts,
he is a good man."

I am, John, recalculating the strategies of change,
re-tooling the weapon of silence.

November 9th, 2016

KD

55.

How far the darkness reaches, wrapping itself around the globe.
All of us implicated, all of us shivering at the prospect.

The rise of fascism on a scale unseen since the 1930s.
The DNA test kits are a quick pick-up on the net.

Whiteness has always been such a strange product –
its many shades wilting in the sunlight but exuding

a poison so toxic it makes heroic couplets sing
with a vision of a future in which anyone

with a gun can claim their little bit of (im)mortality,
their snowflake purity in the furnace of consumerism.

November 10th, 2016

JK

56. as if

On the Election of Donald Trump

For Lorna, Akua and Sena

All night we allow ourselves to play the game show,
to watch the ticking over of numbers, the coloured charts,
the map with blues and reds and shades of pink,
this continent a board game. There are winners
and losers, the ladders and the slithering snakes;
everyone's photo grins. It is as if we have forgotten
that of every one hundred white men, seventy-three
chose the man who sees the bodies of women as a thing
to grab onto, to handle as nothing, the one who laughs
it off, never says sorry, calls it the way of the man, and this
scowling infant of a man, the men have said yes to,
have given him the sceptre and the crown, the command
of their souls – at what price, and to what end? It is as if
we have forgotten that for every one hundred white women,
fifty-three of them have said it does not matter, it is
easy enough to ignore it all, to see in his monstrous ways
something intimate enough to be forgiven, though he has
not asked for it. They have arrived at the terrible sadness
that their daughters' bodies, their sisters' bodies,
the bodies of women who are strangers to them, all
their hard-won dignities: it is as if they do not matter.
He is the father on the Easy Boy, gloating; he is
the pompous chief of the village. There is a language for this –
the language of self-loathing despair. I see my daughter,
my wife, my mother, my sisters, I see their brown bodies
gathered in a corner, their faces full of rightful anger,
and I draw closer, for what I have inside these open
arms is the hollow shelter of one who must wait
for the words to finally find their truest music;
I embrace them; this is an act of prayer, an act

109

of deepest lamentation; an act of solidarity –
that word that means this anger churns in me, too,
and we will let it cut a clear path through the thick
bramble of excuses, justifications, rationalisations
and lies – we will call it what it is, and this,
today, is what we have.

KD

57.

Some weeks ago, before we began our long trek across
Australia and back, before we began to unravel what a trek
actually is and all it implies, a pair of brown honeyeaters
were nesting outside Tim's bedroom window. They
managed to hatch their eggs despite storms and high winds,
only to "fail" at the last, before the chicks had fledged,
the nest brought down by a wild cat. We found it horrific,
and our pity fed back into our selves till we couldn't cope.
Then we hardened ourselves with resolves; almost
separated our selves off. The politics of "nature"
disturbed us. Maybe we over-analysed, but it was
visceral. The traumatised parents going back and forth
to the wreckage of their nest, searching the geranium,
the ground. But since we arrived home, we've watched
the same pair start a new nest in the leafy new growth
of a nearby York gum, out of the reach of cats,
and just now we all stood watching as they unpicked
their old nest and used the strands of grass, web, leaves,
and feathers to augment their new build. They had waited
weeks before trying again. Some would say this doesn't
warrant the term "grieving period", or "recovery time",
but as people who spend much of our lives watching
the creatures we live among, we all beg to differ.
From desolation these birds have risen and are rebuilding
with alacrity and determination. Their curved beaks
are unstitching and restitching; they are alert
and aware of our observation – they observe back,
and we feel the intensity of their gaze. I have less
and less time for analogy and simile, but they
will always be temptation. I can offer something
of these, and this situation. It's hope. A frightening
and damaged word, but still a lever to build with.
Love from us all, my friends, we are with you.

JK

58.

From here, with my eyes in a squint,
and the morning light creating undulations
of shade and sharp edges, the city
can be mistaken for a quarry of rocks
the shades of ochre, burnt sienna, sulphur;
and one could mistake the flat land
edge for the beginning of water.
This is Baltimore, though, and soon
I will descend into the truth of our living –
bodies moving about, leaning against
a wind that has not yet grown cold,
bodies navigating the city with
the casual familiarity of outdoors
people; their coats dark, heavy,
their heads covered, this despite
the sun; it is November, the chill
can fall on you before you expect it.
Here a bit of change is exchanged,
not as a giver to a beggar, but as travellers
trying to make ends meet we look
into each other's eyes. I will admit
that I did not expect to find a wailing
lamentation on these streets, as if
things had changed. It is not cynicism,
it is ordinary memory. "All this anger",
I am told, rushing through the nation,
Trump the conductor of its cacophony.
The mantra is the same: "This is not
America." The thing is, it kind of is,
and that is the sum of it – despite
those who want to think it isn't.
Here, in this city, everything looks
the same, and struggle has a dialect
that still makes sense tomorrow.

Most of us are regrouping, marking
out the terrain, waiting for the invaders,
switching up the street signs,
or just plain taking them down.
Let them relearn the roads, bumble around,
buy us time. From here, we can
see them a thousand miles away. From
here, I like the readable city –
a desert landscape of stones and valleys.
From here, silence is elegant and comforting,
and I wait for the devil to come asking.
"Jump," he says, "and your angels will
catch you." This is hilarious, really,
because I really like it up here,
and I have no idea what he is talking about.
But this is the way things are these days,
we are talking, and fighting and nobody
knows what to call the war.

KD

59.

The sunset is beyond these hills, but amplifies
in orange bands to the west, purple polygons
to the south. The compass is contrary.

But even out in the bush, the poem becomes
a tower. And in my most recent nightmare,
the foyer of the tower was busy with the rich

laughing their way into elevator, doors held open,
laughing with joy as they now have
exclusive access to Hell, which floats

in the imagination like Mars, planet
of war. The business is done. Now
new land-clearing laws mean the bush

of New South Wales will fall to privateers,
to family-orientated expansionists, the dynasts.
I could not escape the foyer,

could not escape outside into clear air
because Escher had become a prophet
of treadmills. Each foyer opened into another,

the only air the air of the airconditioner,
the only "nature" a potted palm
by the concierge's desk. I do not

want to gain the credentials to ride
in those lifts. This pantheist knows
all too well that Hell looks down

on a wasteland, a treeless world
in which sunsets are colour-coded,
where metaphors are the lies of Twitter.

JK

60.

We keep saying history is just
repeating itself, and then wondering

how, because this is a kind of lie,
this repetition; it is only in the way

a grandson looks like his grandfather –
which is as a shadow that invents

new sins because old sins don't work
as they did, and people find old sins

boring. You've got your grandma's eyes,
and the soft belly of your father, and that's why

you are squeamish around blood. So everyone's
looking for a man with a bloody knife –

for the repeating music of history –
while the anti-Christ slips through the grates

of our hearts, and we adore him in spite
of ourselves, because his anus lips have said

he has heart, heart, heart, heart,
and mercy. Which is the language

of despots, how they draw close, breathfully
and say, "Why do you hate me, so? Don't

you know, I love you? Don't you know
I have a gentle hand that can caress you

so you purr with longing?" This is the season
of reinventing reinventions, this is the season

of the shrewd and the greedy, this is the season
of manifestoes of resistance and pamphlets

of protest, this is the season of the deaf,
this is the season of the Deaf Republic.

Says Ilya, my friend, the poet of howls and elegies,
as he signs the simplest sign, "Look!"

And there the gulls make clamour in the eye,
lifting off in one mute cacophony into

the slate grey sky, leaving the water
flat and still, without a trace of their presence.

KD

61.

I went up to the red shed in the mid-afternoon heat
and dragged open the wall-of-a-sliding door and stepped

in to join the spiders and insects. I haven't been in the red shed
for a couple of months and wanted to hear the susurrus

easterly tamping its walls, roof. Outside, hundreds of grasshoppers
leapt against the iron and slid down to repeat, but not wanting in.

Not really. I know that sound. Instinctively, whenever I enter,
I look up into the roof supports to see if a carpet python

has taken up residence, wound its way round. But no.
Though I did see the largest huntsman spider I've

ever seen – it's abdomen as large as a small bird. As
I do with all living things, I watched it watching me,

both on the edge of something completely alien
to the other, only a *folie à deux* of spiritual

residues possible – the all we-are-not igniting
in the warm still life of the shed, that gravid-

barren paradox: rolls of fencewire, remnants
of winter's woodpile, gardening tools, the air

pump for the deep wells we try never to draw on,
the old stable cleaned out and marked by mice.

JK

62.

The air changes when we cross into a new state;
the things we trusted before, we can no longer trust.
We do not know the names of the creatures
trotting across the plains; they move in single file,
all gazing sideways at us, as if about to read who we are.
But "as if" is the evidence of what we do not know,
and we feel relief when they disappear, though the fear
of those creatures that have not come into the open
returns. We received messages that the new leader
of this state praises everyone who enters at the gate;
he says that there is enough food for everyone
and has written many books about the mystery
of the hair of aliens, the entanglements and textures,
a kind of beauty he fears his own people will never
have. Some have said that he is married to a stranger,
but this is a rumour, as those who have seen her
say she looks just like him, and covers her hair,
anyway, so who knows. It is hard to tell when this
country ends, so between us we are agreeing
on the thing that will make us stop and plant
our flagpole and tents. Most of us know that we will
stop when we tire of travelling, but this does not
lend itself to myth, and we know that these myths
will sustain us when the winter comes. So we
are devising the story of our arrival. I have been revising
the tale of the nameless creatures trotting across
the gentle hillside. In my remembering, they formed
a single line and moved in a circle on a piece of land
covered with high grasses, and then kept moving
in circles – I counted one hundred – before stopping
and settling down in a squat. Then they rose
as a host, and sprinted away. As we drew near,
we saw that they had drawn out the plan for a city,
and this is why we settled here. I have not shared

this with anyone yet, because I can't tell yet
whether the creatures were predators or angels,
nor can I say if all they did was piss on the ground,
as lumps of shit would seem a different portent.

KD

63.

Are these the aftershocks, or the creep of tremors
presaging the fall? I stumble about, shuffling,
staring at my feet finding their way over the cracks
opening out in the clay, the laterite soils, almost
overbalancing from rocky outcrop to rocky outcrop.
The bed of grey sand that is the coastal plain
shaken out, salt and pepper down under The Scarp,
the greedy's condiments on their big, eat-all-you-can meal.

But then I regain my footing on hearing my brother
saw a quoll crossing the road near here, near midnight,
then a barn owl fly from one roadside eucalypt to another,
and finally a brushtail possum emerge from riparian
vegetation. I reconfigured. But all of that required
plant-life, and as the large and small, the rare,
fragile and ancient plants now fall down below,
I watch the seismograph in my head morph

a reality I can't own – denying my own sleep.

JK

64.

It seems wrong, a kind of false narrative,
to count by years, ritualising the new year
as if time marks itself in epochs, seasons;
but we are as old as our habits and of those
that came before us, and it is true that rest
arrives only when there is the optimism
of change: a body growing taller, a child
being born, a burial, a season of laughter,
a season of lamentation, a season of the living
and a season of the dead – and here we are,
waiting, oddly, for a new epoch to begin.
What lies ahead is not certain, indeed
it is shadowed by portents of chaos. I have
vowed to read the prophetic books, not in search
of prophecy, but in search of the patterns
of clairvoyance, the music, maybe, of those
locust-eating, barefooted dreads abandoned by all,
so full of the rot of their failings, and so broken
by their flesh, who somehow become holy
in ways that even they cannot grasp, who wake
each morning staring out into the sky
and seeing small glimpses of beauty.
It is true that they can hear in the rustle
of leaves, in the soft wail of wind through
branches and between walls, something
of the way of chaos and decay.
I want to learn how to read the signs,
which is, in its own way, an indulgence,
because I wrote today in a letter that became
a confession, that it is not the unknown
that makes me skittish and smoke-filled,
but the knowing that I labour to deny –
which makes me just like the limping,
half-blind walkers, the ones who know

but deny knowing as a kind of affectation.
When asked, they say what is already there.

You, John, stand before the bulldozer,
for you will not deny the knowing,
you stand among the carcass of trees,
knee deep in the knowing, and you fill
your lungs with the making of indignation,
that breath that turns into a shout
hurled into the void because you will not
allow the indulgence of not knowing.
I envy you this thing which you must
know troubles beauty; and yet, there it is,
the quoll, the owl, the eucalypt, the possum,
the open sky, the pure drunkenness
of seeing, which beauty wrestles, seizes,
overcomes. Which is why I can say,
as if standing on the threshold of a new
epoch, that I wish you vision and beauty,
I wish you joy and laughter, I wish you
the satisfaction of a long sleep at night,
sweetened by the comfort of knowing
that you have done everything you could
to offer our earth's beauty to the world,
against all terror, against all corruption,
against the sharp brandishing white light
of hubris that will be the demon of the season.

KD

65.

The assault on the Beeliar wetlands has shifted gear
south from here – the next section of bushland fenced-off
in extreme heat, animals trapped to perish in agony in sweatboxes.

"Naturalists" employed by government tan their consciences
in this skin-cancer culture and air-conditioners strain like HAL 9000
trying to resolve the contradiction. Red-tailed parrots flame in the fireban.

Bulldozers idle and agitate in their catch-pens, waiting to be let loose.
Here trees fall to illustrate agency of architects and town-planners.
Here trees fall as a contraindication of adrenaline.

Flagging in the heat, protesters and destroyers keep an ear
out for the cricket score, and the summer burns to their core.
The streets surrounding are scenes out of Shakespeare.

We have placed a bowl of water on the verandah
for the family of bobtail lizards that live in a burrow
dug beneath the concrete lip of the verandah, the entrance

covered by a succulent that needs little water, that glows green
in the bake-off that is Industry's gourmet guide to climate.
We are withering here – 44 degrees centigrade

and climbing. The birds struggle to fly beneath
each other, switching sun for shade, feathers casting
with shadows of heartbeats. Echoes of other times.

JK

66.

These small kindnesses and miracles are jewels to secrete
in folds, the cool preciousness of them touching the skin,

a nudge and reminder of how beauty persists in gentler
times: your bobtail lizards grateful for an unexpected swimming hole,

there to sip before the daily oppressions of heat – that is one,
which, of course, I collect with all the hubris of our human art,

a thing in which we have no right to find, except
to observe, deeper meaning for ourselves, like a poem

sent weeks ago by a friend, in which the "you" is me,
unequivocally, which means someone has held me inside,

as one holds hope or prayer for joy deep inside. This is
the sudden pool of water reflecting the blue of an open sky,

there for us to sip. Then the fat language of that succulent,
how much its resilience, its efficiency arrives as a kind of faith

in the way the body is made, how easily this too seems
a tiny burst of verse that delights in the doldrums. The miracle

is to multiply the tiny drops of hope into a satisfying
dampness, the fecundity of our survival, our thriving in the dry

season. This, John, is a roundabout way to say thank you,
and to carry two things close to me for a week and a day,

through a world that sometimes offers such brilliant lights
as the shimmering surface of gently troubled waters.

KD

67.

I've been saving this image, holding it in, a breath
that will renew me when it is released and drawn back:

bees thriving on the algal delta of the leak on the curve
of the great water tank, the only water for a long stretch,

and the bees making the most of it. Renewing to see
them renew, and though we move close, they

are too enamoured of water to bother us.
This, Kwame, is survival, and I've been

holding this back for you because I know
you'll decode into a blueprint for survival

where you are, too. Inauguration day lies
swarm without bees, in a bee-killing

world, the hives diminishing, as you know.
But as the sun roars, here we hear bees, bees.

JK

68.

Someone has promised snow. Outside, in the half light,
I can tell from the heavy sky that the air knows when
the silence will come over us again, and white will
blanket everything. I was not born to snowfall.
Still, I have understood the metaphor of shelter
and how a man, walking out into the evening after
a day in shadow, can be filled with something like hope
at the transformation that snow enacts – a painter
abandoning colour for the shades of grey and light –
the simplicity of it all, and the grand silence.

Yesterday, a man asked me what we are to do,
for something must be done. I told him to do
the things he has always done, and he said it is
not enough to do what he has always done. I
said I would do what I have always done, which did
not please him, for he wanted to change his ways.
I thought to say, "See, there is a small pond
by the roadside, what is stopping you from being
dunked into a new holiness?", but what I said
was nothing. I had nothing to say to him because
I dared not imagine what sins he wanted to set
aside, what inaction he may have regretted. I
continue to do what I have always done, knowing
the old equation of our days. I cast my stones
as one who may be stoned, and each day I shed
the burden of regret, stand on the upturned bucket
and say, "I am the least, and so I can say that beneath
the muting of snow, the worms are simply waiting
for the thaw." This is what I do; I keep the scent
of the cankerworm's efforts in my nostrils. It is
what I must do in the epoch of the mute and the deaf.

KD

69.

Trump need look no further than Australia
for stormtroopers – they are here in ready

supply, keen to hover over borders, less
bird than humans with wings of violent

Northern mythologies. Naming a name – Scott Morrison,
ex-Immigration and Border Protection Minister,

now Treasurer, skites over how America
is catching up to the Australian Way of Exclusion:

so many here quiver with excitement, flags
on their cars, crowing at the cricket,

at the exponential exclusion, the white
dust filling the atmosphere, searching

out skins to redress. So many ready
to accost travellers at airports, to build

walls in and out of imaginations, flatten the bush.
The great unleashing, the bow wows of war,

those nuggety garlands of coo-ees reformatting
language. Yesterday, lightning took out our phone-

connection and left us isolated. That state of mind
on the edge of the range, the great plains stretching.

We have a choice, of sorts, but won't connect
to the National Broadband Network. Won't join in.

And though the NBN's bandwidths lasso
the jamtrees, the monitors, we speak to silence.

JK

70.

Here come the tricksters, fast-talkers, straight-facers,
in their tight trousers, clean suits and worn briefcases;
it is the grand bazaar of the quick fingered, lie-mongers,
stock-answers, with their quick feet, side-changing,
dissembling shit-faces. When you shout, "But it's immoral,"
they say, "Ah, but its legal," and the deep hunger
to be right that covers the nation will nod and nod
and sleep with no fear, for the nice smiles, blond hairs,
neat trims and cool ways have all the farm-talking,
shocked-looking, message-keeping ways of a wall.
It is, of course, the cesspool of power, and the winks
glitter in the screens, and the voices play the jujitsu
of falsehoods. When you wonder out loud, is any
of this real, know that old Derrida, Foucault and Barthes
are lurking in the shadows, a kind of blunt reality
in bedroom slippers and faded pajamas, sipping coffee
and playing with the grandkids, while the world
deconstructs itself around us. Here come the hucksters,
counting their coins, here come the pragmatists
depending on the pushback, here come the harvesters
of all that has been corrupt. It is no myth. The folks
in a moment of calm before the circus of media,
before the buzz of feeds and alerts, stood at the penthouse
of the hotel room, and looked across to the Pentagon,
the open fields of this swamp city, and thought they could
hear the soothing voice say, "Look at all you see
before you…" You know the rest. Nobody jumps, nobody
is a martyr, everyone is a hustler, and will answer
calmly, "Perhaps it is immoral, but our laws must hurry
to meet us before we arrive at the edge of the abyss."
It is not the alarmist who says, "We are there already,
free-falling, free-falling, free-falling." It is the one
who feels the rush of wind in her face, the one
whose stomach lurches; and in our home, we

argue about the colour of cheese, and who said what,
and who cares about whom, as if a contagion
has slipped under the door, doing its slow corrupting.

KD

71.

Sensory overload
reversion
minimalism
distilled –
cherish
the ant on whose desk
crisscrossing workspace
collecting shed skin,
shed pheromones,
marking formic trail
for others to follow,
as easy as Beckett's *Three Novels*
and a name spoken in heat
against a deluge
threatening the dwelling,
concrete foundation
that could shift and float
and slide down the valley face –
digging trenches to ward off
the inevitable; what hermeneutics
work away, the rubble
of shelter:
a question
distilled
minimalism
reversion
sensory overload.

CODA

Reading
the disaster,
now & every-
where.

JK

72.

For weeks I walked my neighbourhood with my dog
as a reassurance to my neighbours that I was not
up to no good, with my head full of Cervantes
in elegant comic translation, while Canada geese
barked across the sky in numbers – refugees
from one ecosystem to another; ah, the open sky
of a novelist's canvas, the beauty of invention,
the healing of invention. Then, somewhere
deep inside a desert of sorts, somewhere in
southern Spain with Africa within earshot,
the scent of that other desert seeping into
Cervantes' colonialist anxieties – where the party
of travellers quarrelled about disguises and the ways
women betrayed men, the codes of honour
and the burning of books – I hungered for other
distractions. I will return to the poet's novel,
knowing now that there is nothing absurd
about the knight errant, nothing comic about
the sincerity of this art of remaking the self
with language. Do I need to point out that
I stopped listening in the middle of that season
of debauched consumption, the festival of the monster
slouching his way to the District of Columbia.
There was no longer a path of escape
in Don Quixote's nobility – it was all becoming one –
and as a respectable citizen I needed a clear
head to witness the inevitable bloodiness
of this nation's wilful undoing of itself. Now,
in the midst of a gloomier place where each day
I contemplate the meaning of happiness, as if
there is a way to understand life through
the examined life, I find myself carrying a sense
of the unfinished sorrow that comes with the life
of migrants like me, who have left homes

we love for places we must learn to love,
or at least tolerate because the homes we love
have betrayed us in ways that only love
can betray. We will always carry
in us an unfinished music, a sense that perhaps
if we returned to that hollow we might find
the beginning of beginnings – that thing I have
called salvation most of my life, that thing
of tender nostalgia. I don't have to say it, do I,
that I know this to be its own kind of myth,
that I know that a therapist might plant a flag
inside every person's insides called "longing",
and there release a swarm of lethal insects
we could call the "what might have beens"? You and I
know that it is not the need to return in time –
that is not the poet's most useful hunger –
but a need to repeat the settled ease of words
caught right and told beautifully in all things.
We are refugees of beauty, which we can't
admit to a world where men and women
are suffering separation, homelessness, threats
of death, hunger, and loss. But to you, John, I can say
that the woman waiting for a visa, permission
to live another day, when she is silent deep
in the night, when she is testing the groans
inside her, when she has prayed and is waiting
for the dark to speak back, it is that elusive
thing, that beauty, the longing that she knows
she has lost, it is this, that makes her weep.
It is this that makes her sing softly the song
that only she knows as a comfort. Every time
I write a poem, I find myself trying for that song;
this is the gap that seems to grow every time
we pour more words into its consuming maw.

KD

73.

As said, I can't enter the country where my son was born, where I lived
with my family for five years, unless I am given a special waiver.
This can take nine months to process, so I can prove myself
worthy of visitor's rights. Those old protests seem
more topical than ever. If ground's worth protesting on,
then even as the ground slips from beneath our feet
the need to protest remains and grows stronger.
Now, I guess, not even a waiver would
be possible. The doors are closed.
My next book of poetry is to be called
Open Door Policy, and this was before
the latest inflections of xenophobia rolled
back humanity into its bank accounts, religious
portfolios, or lack thereof. I sit in a carpark
in the town of Northam, wheatbelt Western
Australia, and even this moment is a protest.
I won't situate myself on the other side of the shops
where old-growth marri trees high as highrise buildings
were chopped down to make way for carpark solar panels.
My protest was met with, "This is an act of sustainability".
The short circuit, the errant schematics, and the names
of so many species left out of the language tree.
But I have no authenticity. And I have no biography.
I am not vatic though I know, against summer's severity,
the banks of the river are close to bursting and we know
this is the way of it now: evaporation, deluge, scorched earth —
a new kind of emptiness that defies the will to return
the sign to its origins, its custodians. But I will
count on hearing the strange nightflights of corollas
again over the coming week, against the grain,
unusual, reconfiguring. Reconfiguring, a word
I lapse into or look to or find necessary
with increasing repetition. I will draw
images of flight I can't see in my notebooks,

I will deploy colours I don't know. Whole
new ant empires have set root hereabouts,
after the deluge's softening up. Doors
are straining on their frames with the shift.
We wish to keep them open, to the air, to new-
comers. Those systems that close give no fertility,
and genetically modified canola is the death
of the future – as much as wounds hacked
into diminishing bushland. Poets,
deny advertising the hooks
of language. Poets,
forget about each other's
status and let the language
rush together. We know this, Kwame,
I am sure we do. This conversation,
like so many other conversations, a lens
to what we utter ourselves,
what we let ourselves hear.
Listen, listen, the corollas
are rolling in early, up from
the paddocks, into the flooded gums
down in the valley, soon towards us,
towards us all, becoming those species
you know, who won't be pinned to their genus.
And the ground will be baked hard
again soon, so soon.

JK

74.

The cataracts, I am told, are mild, but there –
enough to let me contemplate the craft
of replacing my lens with a neat plastic disc,
beneath the intact corneas borrowed from a dead
boy who theology can't vouch will not demand
them back in the sweet by and by. Something that will
sharpen my sight, ensure thinner spectacles,
which, the logic goes, will increase my options
for seeing in the dark. These eyelash growth-
drops, though, must be my daily ritual until
death ("for the rest of your life," he said,
with the calm of one who has planned out
the years left tightly – so little time left) to
slow the petrification of muscles behind
my creaturely bulbs. So I laughed as Sarah
did when the call came in for a new round
of trials with contacts. "We are hopeful,"
the perky attendant said. "The doctor thinks
the new protocols are promising." Ah the pain
of hope, and the terror of faithlessness. Still,
that time it worked out well – a ninety-year-
old woman waddling around pregnant
and proud, spitting, no doubt, a torrent of bile.
There are no glorious hymns of thanksgiving
in Sarah's legacy, just the litany of regrets
and resignations. She makes the best patron
saint of accidental grace: "Just a part of the plan,
you know, and don't worry, I am happy
to be alive, ha ha ha!" It is hard to know this,
but I began this as a song of thanksgiving
for the post-winter solstice, the strange bauble
of sweetness at the spread of light at dawn
earlier these mornings, even in the midst
of the fog of our days. I had laughed out

the laugh of the man who discovers that still
the back of his right ear is ticklish – how lovely!
Which means laughter dries up quickly,
for fear that that nerve, too, will deaden
if overused. I am comforted by what I can
smell in the air – the animal rawness of our
elusive earth. Now, more than ever,
I have no way to process the myth of dominion,
the idea that I can tame what rolls across
my eyes – the sky grand as the future.
It will outlast me, this I know, and sometimes
this is the only scale I can carry in my head,
tomorrow and tomorrow, creeping pettily.

KD

75.

Sight. So vulnerable, taking so much craving
for layout, colouring in, delineation. Exposure.

Today, I was among the rough-barked trees,
aware that a sleeping tawny frogmouth

was near. For ten years I've been keeping
an eye out, scanning the twisted and bent

branches, half hoping to see the daysleeper.
At night, coming in late, we sometimes witness

a pair in the headlights rising up to those
branches, taking us all in, gulping light

in their upset shapes. And today, I am sure
I did see, did make out a form: beak,

eye, tail-feathers. And an egg shell
cast to the ground, a species identifier.

And overhead, a nankeen kestrel fast
with the valley's upswing as storms

approach again. Then I take
these sights indoors, lay them out

polarised to recollect, the glow
a trick of perception, the real

world we need to imagine.
And then, and then. And now.

JK

76.

These days I lecture on the past like a prophet,
leaving potent herb seeds in the earth, never
sure how fertile the ground is. I carry
in my head the scrolling narrative before us,
such that when I say, "Follow the money,
do not be distracted by the emotion of words
that have been freighted with such angst,
like racism. Just follow the money and the religion
of success; only then can you know our
corruption." I say this about the carpet-
baggers ranging across Manning County
with their quick tongues and northern ways,
in the blighted aftermath of that war, where
persistent fires still burn on the battle grounds,
and the stench of the dead has not quite lifted.
I am laying the rough path into our present
moment, and my students do not nod, they
carry that blank gaze of these mid-western
people of stoic calm. Who knows if it would be
better for me to leap on the desk and shout
in the cadence of a truly holy man, funky
with righteousness, "Hey, the Scripture says
to Pharaoh, 'I yanked you up for this very
reason, for this true intention, that I might
show off my power in you – yes, you;
and that my name might be shouted all
across this land, all across the world!'"
The trick here is hubris – how the servant
of the most diabolic constructions might
imagine himself a chosen one. Who will
ask me, in the interim, about the theology
of violence, the collateral damage of The Plan,
the necessity of a heavenly home, for any
of this to sound like a comfort to us?

Instead, I rehearse the corruptions of the past,
and trust in the comforts of repetition.
For every disaster, there is a blue print
to its making, and maybe knowing this
is all that can be asked of the Scripture.

KD

77.

In the building where egrets fly past high but at eye level,
electric lights mark the river where litmus paperbarks once pumped
the coats of painted water into layers of skin, peeling with sunset.

In the building where egrets fly past high but at eye level,
and the nearby zoo strains to keep its ark status, savannah animals
call out against the trade winds, refuse to agist to traffic.

In the building where egrets fly past high but at eye level,
phases of your life shift to match the trail of decades,
no one able to fully squeeze you out with their landscaping.

In the building where egrets fly past high but at eye level,
you are hemmed in by building regulations relaxing to the tune
of developers and "river views", though many will see less and less

as a consequence, and flight paths will tighten, and inside we'll adjust?
In the building where egrets fly past high but at eye level.

JK

78.

Soon the people forgot everything.
The women saw his pouting lips
and caught the sweetmeats that fell
from them and imagined them jewels.

If you squat and shit out rubies,
opals and onyx stones, this magic
will turn your asshole into a relic
of faith. This is all an illusion,
of course, but people have dreamed
of less and lived in joy for months.

Every battered person knows
that their greatest guilt and shame
is the emptiness they feel when
the beating stops. This, too, is an
illusion, but the little boy sold
his cows for a handful of coloured
beans and he ran home rejoicing.

The two women on the canvas
are forgetting their nakedness
because they are forever in repose —
and the truest art lies in the muddy
palette that made them. All illusions.

The despot has given us the language
of relief. He smiles and says heart,
as a doctor would say to you, "Your heart, sir."

Where is the monster we imagined?
Lurking in the shadows. Look closely
into the brown gloom behind the women!
He is there, this is the truth, well-dressed

and gloating. Soon the people forget
what is coming; it is the art of silence.

The despot feeds on the lull
in the air, he grows fat.

KD

79.

I drive Tim through a riverside zone
where bush thrived when I was a child.

On the radio is a Debussy piano piece –
"L'isle joyeuse", which the announcer

says is about Watteau's painting
L'Embarquement pour Cythère.

The announcer is uncritical in this declaration.
The announcer is enamoured of revellers

having been on the island of Venus,
missing the point that they are leaving.

Debussy might have been speaking
to something completely different.

And in describing what was here –
the tangled ranks of skin-hanging

paperbarks, the deep-seeking flooded gums,
and further out from the riparian with its subtexts of reeds,

marri gums and overlit banksias – I am thinking
of a different array of imagery. Having no choice,

in distress, but to see the bare bones of thinned sands,
the freeway surmounting lavish mountains

gauche as galleries. Paintings designed for mansions.
The art we hide behind. The tree a sculpture

that can't be bettered in the landscaping.
The moon-disk jellyfish thrown on a jetty

to set like ghosted quartz under the harsh sun –
a peculiar and cruel revelry set against a hierarchy

of nervous systems. And the pelican
circling in time with pulsating joggers,

and cars tipping into exuberant redness, braking
to slow for traffic calming, making the river

something it isn't, a place for reflection, art and muzak:
the lore and codes rewritten in essence.

JK

80.

Words betray me, they haunt me, they leave me
with the illusion of truth. I am drowning in the persistence
of the words written down, kept for decades,
returned to as if returning to all truth. After all,
what is true is what we remember, and suddenly
what we remember is overwhelmed by what is written,
and how quickly what is written fills the gaps,
the things forgotten. I am speaking of love,
I am speaking of the persistence of narratives,
I am speaking of the curse of language – the use
of language. Often she has said, "You are different
because you are a poet", and I, feeling wholly
useless and base in my instincts, flawed and lost,
fat and incapable of discipline, protested,
called it a myth. I have no special dispensation,
and nothing is known about me, truly known
about me by understanding me to be a poet.
As with most things, silence followed, the weighty
silence of disagreement. But I am drowning
in words, the words I have kept, as if perhaps
by keeping them I will understand memory,
and the cliché of mortality and immortality
explains their attraction. I am, these days,
purging memory by purging the words,
the sheets of paper, the narratives. I do wonder
whether contentment comes from the balm
of forgetting. I do wonder this, even as I write
this down too. Still, what we do here, what
we hold in these moments, carry
the substance of language – bear witness to
our epoch of deafness and wounding,
and even as I jettison the messy past, I retain
its filtered remnant, the language strained
of the superfluous hiccups of our days. I now

have a reason to do this thing, which perhaps,
is as ordinary as new mornings, but it is what
I present as a greeting across time, across worlds.

KD

81. "Boosh"

The world I inhabit with my family and others
who feel the pain of destruction is unravelling.

Tim and I watch forests decorated with pink
and blue and yellow ribbon fall day after day –

the war brought home from the bare plains
of the Flat Earth Society whose science

is the technology of consumerism and not
knowledge that illuminates a way between

ancient trees without burning them down. And today
a guy is jailed for bashing a kangaroo to death

with a crowbar after tormenting it, summoning
his mate who is filming on his "smart phone",

Come down into the death zone, come on, mate –
throwing stones, goading the dog on, the roo

up to its chest in a dam, ochre water. The taunting
and rushes of blood, the call from mate to mate:

'Boosh' it! Hashtag horror in the cauldron
of data, the crashing pastoral lapped up

like a promise of "boosh", the hard times
made up for by the land handing itself over?

JK

82.

"...place is messy"
    — Kei Miller

Briefly, as they say in Leeds, the sky left me
bewildered, like an alien trying to decipher
the noises in the air. There is a heaviness
that comes with being a stranger, until one
surrenders to the dialect of tones – as if reading
the language of birds and wind and the sky.

The sky in Leeds crowds in, consumes space,
carries the quality of tumult and constant action,
as if portending doom. All of this, I admit,
in contrast to the flat, post-apocalyptic glare
of the Nebraska sky – this is how it seemed
before all things, and after the cataclysm.

Either way, the sky teaches us how to prophesy
the end of the world. My native tongue is the epic
un-scrolling above the Blue Mountains, so that we
in the foothills, on the plains of Mona, would constantly
look to the hills to read our fate. I once lay stretched
out on a Saturday, on a clay-caked cricket pitch,

and read the sky, the chase and swirl, the deep
hues and light filigree of wispy clouds, and soon
I could predict the arrival of storm. This gave me
comfort, a kind of peace, for I knew in nineteen seventy-
seven, that a powder house would explode; I knew,
well, Paul's calm celibacy of devotion, that this world

in its present form was passing away, and under
the deluge, I prayed in sobbing thanksgiving, for – as if
magic had happened here – I could tell the storm

would arrive, even when the sky seemed disinterested,
and knowing this, this sense of sure doom was a comfort.
For the first time I believed I had arrived in a native place.

KD

83.

Near death. Close to disaster. These epithets
come about for reasons and who am I to abandon
them in a time of tension, a time of broken language?
Driving with Tim on Eadine road at 8.46 this morning
a roo – a doe – leapt across the road faster
than I've ever seen a roo move, and that's fast.
I hit the brakes and grazed its tail as it raced
across our line of vision, and though it was okay,
and so were we, it was close, really close.
I have hit a roos in cars before and it's devastating –
as a child, sulking in the footwell of my father's car,
we struck a roo and the car crumpled around me.
About eight years ago, driving with our daughter,
a roo was chased by hunters onto a nightroad
and the impact was redefining. Roo destroyed,
car written-off. I wrote about that to expunge
the trauma, to reassemble fragments of shock,
of exclamation, of lost phonemes. I write again
for the same reason, though the damage this time –
on the surface at least – was minimal. But that doe
was escaping something, and there was terror
in its leaps. No doubt shooters. No doubt, really.
I keep writing these things because this is what
poetry is to me – not exoneration or relief,
but witness and recounting, a haphazard recounting
that shapes and tries to find a way out. There's
nothing worth displaying here, nothing
worth separating off as art. It's just blunt
and brutal and distraught and amazed.
Tim said the roo made larger leaps
than he's ever seen a roo make before, turning
itself into a blur, leaving us far behind.

JK

84.

for Derek Walcott

"...For no matter how many promises God has made, they are "Yes" in Christ. And so through him the "Amen" is spoken by us to the glory of God." Paul (2 Cor. 1:20)

In the black box, the lights isolate emotion
with theatrical efficiency; every gesture is art,
as if in the clean, rehearsed moments, the word
as the beginning of all things, and glorious yes
of possibility, must be followed by the congregants
saying Amen. This is the holy theatre, a world
I have come to think of as a home place, a shelter,
the womb of my art. So there in that black box
deep inside a winter storm in Providence, they
tell me the old man has slipped into his first sleep,
and his editor calls each day to listen to the soft
ebb and flow of the sea in his breathing. No one
wants to say "All is silence now", but we do know
that after the poem is over, what remains is a soft
pulse of the sea where we, the Makaks of history,
find our cathedrals, our history, our glorious tomb.
I did not expect the thickening pain in my throat,
as if I could fall down and weep. I did not expect
the moment to be like this, but it was, and here
is the beginning of our lamentation. For weeks
I have carried in my head the calculation of greatness –
how ambitious was the madman Lowell, how
full of the privilege of his New England elitism,
how it is that every time I read of the Boston police
coming to secure him and carry him to another dark
asylum, I can only think that I envy him the dignity
they afforded him; and I think that the St. Lucian
would have known that five white Boston cops

would not have sat at his breakfast table while he shivered
and ranted and read for them "The Sea is History",
before escorting him to the asylum of fire and healing.
This is the way history arrests ambition. We stay
sane so that we can live to go mad in our secret chambers.
But the old man has slipped into his first sleep and at last
all his promises of last poems, last words, last
testaments, seem fulfilled. This is not yet an elegy, merely
an effort to clear the phlegm in my throat, and a way
of saying that this art comes to us burdened with
so many yeses and nos, and on this morning of grey
chill, I have learned to pray for language, just enough
to offer a word of company for the old man. The word
is waves – not original, surely, but I offer it – the sea,
the soft waves reaching the coast, the pulling back,
the soft snore of a man waiting to leave the shore at last.

KD

85.

Chuck Berry is performing "Johnny B. Goode".
He dies. He dies while I am listening.
I find out later, but not much later.

And Walcott dies, and lines from *Omeros*
flow through the valley, inland, far
away from their beaches, coastline.

They flow beyond copyright,
beyond quoting rights, looping across
the oceans of time to the Odyssey.

Chuck Berry was said to be
a difficult man. Keith Richards worshipped
his "licks". We are of them. Islands. Atolls.

The uncanny shatters the red sands here
and they rise up to orbit my life, so distant.
But not like space junk – more like

planets waiting to form. None
of this can be taken, or marketed –
the outrageous, the riotous, the forbidden.

Whose testament collects in these branches –
nightbirds and daybirds colluding, sharing?
Such meditations on breaks of sound
        and light.

JK

86.

i.

Every image seems taken on this island,
devoured by that dead poet's eye,
and even this lament is a cliché
other poets have complained before.

We come through a column of clouds;
the jet shudders as if something muscular
has troubled it, before we break
into that light over the sea – the two mountains.

ii.

I leave Lorna a message, another insult
I plant on my skin, because I have no language
to explain that after we ask for love
what we get is a second thought.

"You think too much," the hot wind
mutters, and I say, "It is my age now,
I have grown soft." I know that every mercy
I receive is a second thought. The days

when I was the first thought are over,
and I must learn a new way to tease
the hunger that turned affection into
a fever, a kind of obsession, maybe love.

iii.

In the dream two poems are laid out
side by side. It is near a beach, and air
clicks to insects; someone is explaining
the edit of a famous poem: "See, here

he chops out this long shimmering list
of colonials, old lovers, enemies, and ghosts,
five lines of iambics sparkling with colour
before the summation, 'my wounds' – which he keeps."

iv.

I have come to mourn the old man;
I know that his Boston students are in tropic
black, veils of Dickinson's fashion, and how
they cross their legs and weep. It is love

that makes them weep, the secret bubble
a poet can plant in a heart, a naming of desire.
They will miss this, they will know to cry;
it is part of the epic they are writing inside.

I know that if I tear, it will be for my father
again, the world I lost so many years ago;
this is the only language of loss I can read now,
that and hers, the merciful giver of second thoughts.

v.

I do not trust my words these days —
we must call it a crisis. Each day it is as if
I have arrived at a cesspool of feeling
that covers me with the reek of disquiet.

I rehearse a new way to haunt her,
there is no script, really, just a shuffling of cues;
perhaps this way, not that way, or maybe
if I start here, then she… I do not trust my words.

vi.

Izzy, my taxi driver is an ex-cop — six five,
slender as a fast bowler. He tells me about
dead-reckoning, about the sexton, about
the starboard and port, about the treachery

of night boating, how on the sea the darkness
can overwhelm you. I can't help myself, of course,
every thing is a stolen metaphor here,
and I am lost, waiting for some wreckage to wound

the dumb belly of my vessel. "Out there,
you do what you can to avoid water," he says.
My stomach aches these days, as if I am waking
to the night's news that sleep was merciful to.

vii.

I want to tell Robert of a scheme I have devised.
Already, I know it sounds absurd, but I still
arrange it in my head. Let's travel this island
and turn it into a walking monument for the poet,

with plaques, embossed with his lines, so that
pilgrims can receive this place as if it has belonged
at least to the most elegant genius of a poet,
and they will come. Then I think of how easy

it is to speak this way of a strange country, how
easy it is to colonise someone else's home;
after all, Walcott was right about Marley
owning the mountains of Jamaica, and more right

that the mountains of Jamaica owned Marley,
that we offer merely the second thoughts of love,
we come to these places of green riot begging
for love, and our poems are consumed by the twilight.

Castries, St. Lucia

87.

With a death we write about light –
what choice do we have but to
write about the light of a slender 'l',
the dark of a broad 'l' – in a name,
in a description of place filled
with fragments of language?

Tracy tells me about pronunciations
and dialects, about the workings
of the tongue as we cross from language
to language. This is what she does,
drawing words across polylingual strings.
Here, singers whose songs wove

themselves into the land are listening
as their words are brought back,
remade in the shape of country.
It is astounding and illuminating
to witness – to hear – from a periphery,
no, much further out than that, from without.

I am thinking outside you, Kwame,
on the island of the dead poet, a poet
weaving the water, the soil, the vegetation
into an elegy – I can't separate
the living from the dead and can't
be part of the moments. But I feel, I do.

I grow lonelier, Kwame, on the edge
of the valley, watching a family
of black-faced cuckoo shrikes
come back into this part of their range,
moving daily from juvenile to adult,
still enravelled in each other's emergence.

Soon it will get territorial. As with the red-capped
robins and the rufous whistlers, and all the colour-codings
of observation and recordings, shoring ourselves
up against fragility, inevitable loss. Water here
moves deep underground, under a hundred
metres of granite and red soil, bloodier

as it diminishes. The fusing of elegies,
these outriggers to loss. Your being where
you are, Kwame, is an intervention
into loss for all of us. I didn't know
the prophet of St Lucia, but I did know
his words, read here in the wheatbelt. Almost
        understood.

JK

88.

As if it knows already the map to the end,
my body breaks down slowly – each sharp
fearful vision eats at flesh – a kind of canker;
and who will write the elegy that said,
like autopsies should say, "This is how he went;
it was too much." Those who live beside
rivers deep in the jungle territories, who stand
by the water each day and see the erosions
of time, they can carry in their heads both
the catastrophes of time, and the timelessness
of a river flowing on beyond us. They know
each day what they will leave behind; and they
eat fish from the river poisoned by the river's
dying, and they wet their feet in the water,
and they stand and stare into skies loud
with their vernacular, and imagine what remains.
They, I fantasise, are those who understand
the erosion of their bodies. It is a myth,
a kind of envy, but perhaps that is the way
of dreams, and the way we survive our fears.
The old man in his snobbery declared,
"How can anyone be a poet and hate the water,
hate the sea?" One day, he read Césaire,
heard his prayer, "Make me the executor
of these masterpieces", and he knew that black
man was looking at the shape of his island,
and praying for language. He, too, prayed for this.
I know that home is not my territory; I have
no land to call home, and I return only to love,
this woman who said, "If I had a choice of plenty
without you or scarcity with you,
I'd choose to be with you. So I still chose you."
My body reversed its decay at once; I rose
in the dark, my eyes stinging, my throat

full of the sweet pain of homecoming. I am
standing at the edge of water, staring
into the land and waiting for the creatures
to name themselves, waiting for the language
of trees, and grass, and bush, and earth,
waiting to name things that have had their
own names forever; all because this traveller
has, even for an instant, been told that love
waits for me somewhere. We are, John,
marking out the reason for our art – for why
we continue to do this; at least so it seems
to me, and I am left with the most ordinary
of things: the unasked-for hand on my lower back,
resting there, as if it owns me, fully owns me.

KD

89. symploce

Night brings dramatic shifts in perception out here as many night
creatures roam closed and opened spaces making their day.

Night is not a polarisation nor a cancelling nor an adding up nor an
expectation nor a necessity nor an absolute nor a hymn nor an
elegy for day.

Night brings terrors you won't expect and we might talk them off but
a twig breaking doesn't reset and it's irrelevant tomorrow will be
a different day.

Night stresses loss and I think over the praise I offered up to the great
Omeros and the lukewarm re the *Hound* and I am disturbed into day.

Night is brazen and I am fearless for others who know under the cloak
they will be taken away and sunrise will collapse into day.

Night disposes night repossesses night roams night tamps down
edges night is disrupted by phosphorescence in a rough inland sea
and claims day.

Night turns translations back into originals and turns originals back
into utterances and back into thought and masquerades as dreams
of day.

Night is when I couldn't sleep for decades and memorised long
poems which I played back against the back of my eyelids brighter
than red day.

Night transfigures none of grief in itself but wears it down to
filaments of exposure of aperture and light locks onto films of
memory of your day.

Night moths against the window want to eat light though it will
   mean their demise and butterflies pinch-shut their wings waiting
   for day.

Night doesn't suit your eyes our eyes not completely and it will cost
   you it will cost us a planet to make our nights your endless day.

Night is no more illuminating for the dead than it is for the living, but
   then again, then again, then again, what do you get out of day?

Night-painting isn't an array of collectors pinpointing the age of stars
   and galaxies and black holes giving nothing back but hope of day.

Night isn't a diurnal-longing to thrive in a realm of vitamin D and to
   catch a future in the sharp reflection off sand that is the glass of day.

Night has let go of me, Kwame, and I read of a singer vulnerable in
   the shade of his love for heaven and earth and rosy-fingered dawn.

JK

165

90.

Deep in this morass of petty narratives,
I can't imagine a time when I was not swirling –
when I had a cocksure ease with living,
the body moving through dreams fearlessly.
What I am saying is that inside my head
are plots and subplots; they twist and turn,
full of betrayals and revelations,
and were this a lark, I would not wake at three
feeling as if I am dying – my throat pulsing,
my mind battered by the shattering confession –
all lies, all lies, all lies. This is a kind of madness,
and I should be a novelist, someone who can
trade in the intrigues that haunt me. I have
learned the trick of survival – the calm, flat voice
of an actor reading someone else's fiction,
and though sometimes distracted by a freight
train trudging up Antelope Parkway – those
bright yellow skins in the spring rain – leaving
this small gap for me to quickly construct
yet another invention of loss – a late twilight
afternoon, two bodies in shadow at opposite
ends of a corridor, moving towards each other
in tears (it's all melodrama, of course), saying,
"Why, why, why?" This is how the stories
come, how they go. Still I can be drawn back
by the inventions of others. I turn the headphones
up, batter my brain and, this way, I have
a small spot of peace before my insidious
plots start again. I will never write these down,
for these are fictions only in the truest
sense, things I fear can happen, things
I keep inventing out of neurosis. I am a cliché,
and I would offer nothing alarming to a psychologist –
which is somewhat embarrassing. There is,

though, just the slightest sense of hubris
in knowing that I carry in my face the ease
of a man so fully assured of himself, he appears
to have anticipated every barking goose
needling the sky. Nothing surprises him.
All lies, of course. And so, here is how I fall
asleep, at last, each night: I say to myself,
"Imagine, man, the worst," and I do, and grow nauseous,
and feel something like death coming on me,
and then, body limp and useless, I drift.
It helps, of course, that we are listening
to the Book of Leviticus on tape each night,
the voice of God like a confirmation of all that
is unknowable in the here and now. Yes,
this, too, makes me sleep a kind of holy sleep.

KD

91. polysyndeton and crown decline

Wandoo crown decline is upon us with a vengeance and seeing swathes
of lush foliage become switches of dead leaves

and dead branches, and mirrors to living clumps of surviving foliage and
harbingers of the great ghostly trees' collapse

into the shift we won't arrest, saying we can't and it's gone too far and
the story has changed so much and that all growth

is in retrospect and is memory and is nostalgia and balance has been
tipped; no, no, no; if the condition of our admiration

is shade, if the condition of our appreciation is the forms of wood, if the
condition of our wonder is the dynamics of light

playing off yellow-orange bark of spectra of day all-weather paint to
draw out flushes and clot of smooth flows of sap

to link across to capillaries and vessels of our own inclusiveness, what
we'd take out of the completeness of presence

we feel we can lock onto: generational presence becomes an off-the-
rack, ready-to-wear claim to being here with accoutrements,

all of the tales blurring together as if the tall boats brought in the ancient
ways and the ghosts were already tilling the soil (ineffectively);

and. and. and; and now we follow tarmac impositions, desire-lines
agreed upon, survey produce schematics and see the wandoos'

loss of canopy the crowning glory of edging and hedging and lopping-
off bets to meet the urge of every capitalist

self right(eous) auditor serving the self-serving, the get ahead at all costs
the liberty to fruit where eucalyptus caps are dead

before separation, before opening filaments, before parrots can make
feathers shine, glory-be, through ingestion and take stock

and take windmill water from aquifer propping up land's thirst and dust
rolling as metaphor and museum-theft data hunger.

Wandoo crown decline is upon us with a vengeance and seeing swathes
of lush foliage become switches of dead leaves

and dead branches, and mirrors to living clumps of surviving foliage and
harbingers of the great ghostly trees' collapse.

JK

92.

Sun days. Chill air. Sun days. Chill air. A body
moves out of the shadows, searching for sun.
Sun days. They arrive with surprise. A body
has been practising the dialect of sorrow,
and this light, tender as early dusk light,
suggests a smile, a healing smile that floods
everything. Sun days. Chill air. Sun days.
I fear the path to words – they are hanging
over me, these twisted sounds seeking something
like answers, although what they do want
is a narrative that welcomes the days that follow.
It is spring time here in Nebraska. They
tell me the cranes are prancing in the Platte
basin, moving with prehistoric elegance.
So old here, even our bodies feel like alien
creatures; the flat prairie consumes everything;
only ancient things make sense here. The rains
will come each day, spot the concrete roads,
and the governor says the prairie will feed
the world – corn, wheat, and cattle –
for the water table's deep and endless,
the people industrious in the flat
silence of these lands. Here, optimism
is celebrated in quiet nods; the chemicals
seep deep into the earth, and soon we will know.
Sun days. Chill air. Sun days. Chill air.

KD

93. Inside Turner's Sunrise With Sea Monsters

'The Sun is God!'

— said to be Turner's last words

I have seen these monsters pulling down boats
when the sun switches current, shock
to the system mocking darkness, which far
beneath will be anyway, and red tails
form an idea of threat, a brilliant
end lost to the net of critics.

I have seen these monsters pulling down boats
when the sun switches current, behaving
in what they know and are compelled
to do, mast down in the sea receiving
signals across fused states
separating as the sun rises.

I have seen these monsters pulling down boats
when the sun switches current, salt and vapour
wisping away, breaking in and out of focus
to confound senses and make that life-
after-death truth of immolation, a watery
grave or the fluids of rebirth.

I have seen these monsters pulling down boats
when the sun switches current, staring
long enough at their movements, their
actions becoming part of their scenario.
Who is to blame? Who is to survive?
Who is to record what we witness?

JK

94.

'Love's breath is spare'

— Jay Wright

Here the voice is revered – the low notes,
the ones the best singers hold, throats
relaxed, articulation clean as country
night – the rumbling of sorrow or desire.
Here the poet longs for the crescendo,
for the rising action of emotion, for
the way it shapes a room, turns it
into a ship caught far out at sea, all
turmoil and bravery, the kind of faith
that trusts the stars and the markings
on maps. I do not know this place,
except as one who has imagined it
through its poet's music; through
the tragedy of his early death; through
the echo of his voice in the poets
I have copied for their reach – grand,
sloppy, full of passion and full of wounds.
Which means I do not know this place,
except as one who lives in words,
lives in the sound of green, grey
angst, sinfulness, delight, grace,
and sudden alarm at the instant
something unexpected arrives – a stroke
of light inside a swirl of grey shadows,
or a colour – amber or burnt sienna –
warm against the grey and the green,
or perhaps ordinary notes, daisies
on a small patch of grass. We are
together in Swansea, and there is love
here, spare and reliable, and there

is too, the clean, humble exuberance
of Thomas, his voice hurtling above
the old mossy prison walls, the age
they have preserved by calculated neglect.
It will be a day of soft light,
and deepest silence, and this
will be enough for us, enough indeed.

KD

95.

'It is time to rewrite the history of darkness'

— Jay Wright

In this hemisphere, the windrows are alight
and thunderheads of carbon hang heavy
against a stark blue sky. Even now, at a time
when chemical fertilisers burn the soil
against the grain, saturate with nitrogen
and trace elements, the "earlier" ways
are clung to – a double dose
and everything burning, and what
won't fall to "escaped" flames – say a tall
York gum studded with nests – is toppled
with a digger or whatever heavy machinery
the farmer can lay hands on. You see,
after the burning and the cooling of the soil,
dry seeding will begin as an invocation
of rain. Hubris or wishful thinking or a scattering
of seed into alien earth, into stuck parables,
and all those farmroads and mainroads
laid over tracks from waterhole to waterhole,
when burning was to promote fresh green growth.
And now. And now. Under recharted stars,
Milky Way robbed of fertility, the growth
will be GM canola or a flush of weeds
to be struck stonedead showing their faces.
I grew up with a mechanic's understanding
of ballbearings and grease and gearing.
And even with this knowledge I choke
as the flames eat up the stubble and chaff.
And the flames mess with the star charts,
though the Southern Cross shouts its kangaroo-head
name, and an emu thrashes against barbed wire.

I listen hard against the feathering night,
the sun's residues acrid in my mouth,
struggling for clean air, for the insight
of Jay Wright's poem of night and history.

JK

96.

"Pots treat me kindly, fall with a logical
flow. Some I know will cunningly play with my
head, flare and turn, a nesting sorrow,
set near the hearth of my spirit's corner."

— Jay Wright

In another poem, a man dreams of a time
of remembering – twenty years after the sickness
of betrayals, acrimony, and that long nervy
period of purgation, the tense détente when love
is a grassy no-man's land, only entered
during feast days when the ritual acts of peace
allow us to think of hope – a future. In his
poem, there is an image of a couple in comfort,
a quiet affection, a treasured thing, he says.
And reading this, I think that one of us will sit and stare
at the blighted dogwood and wonder about
the what-if of early death. This is as morbid
as the prophet who, in a moment of quiet,
when God has gone silent – rummaging
through some old papers on his desk
to find the thing he meant to say but had
somehow forgotten – so many distractions –
sits and wonders whether she will be remembered
for the things predicted that came to pass,
or for the brief arias of hope, streaks of light
against the gloom – the empty barns, the rusty
fields, the wounded sky, the cracked earth,
the barren olive tree. "But," she says, "God will
bless you…" The pots are aligned before me,
terracotta pots turned down to the ground,
their wombs swirling with the echoes of my

future. I am to choose, one after the other,
the reckoning. Turn them over, and wait for news.
I will always be turning over the pots,
rows and rows of them, stretched as far as I can see
over the open ground; and even knowing
that I have no control of what seethes inside
these gives me no comfort, just the hunger
to keep trying. I come from places
where turned-down pots mean magic,
mean hidden things, mean spirits
waiting to speak or, having spoken, mean
there is something beyond me. It is an uneasy
thing not knowing, and yet how dreadful
the thought of knowing, how terrible
the weight of that burden. I have one
answer: the prophet will be remembered
for speaking what she does not know,
and knowing she will be long dead
even as the knowing is revealed on the earth.

KD

97.

'acacia for the veins of my hearth'

— Jay Wright

Wright's dedication to *Explications/Interpretations*
is "For Harold Bloom and Robert Hayden".
I note this because it is relevant in exponential ways –
a mixture of vision and pragmatism, of past and future.
The morphemes of 'The Continuing City: Spirit and Body'
riffle through my sense of here – relatively isolated,
the town about fifteen ks away, using carnivorous
scents to attract visitors, then wanting them gone.
A town, not a city, applying the filters, regulating
power wired over from the regional centre, Northam,
which in turn receives it from southern power stations.
The library in this house, at this place we name
after a local species of acacia – a name
that can only be temporary, only mark
our presence not ownership – the library
in this house is full of many voices in many languages
and those languages crosstalk, and I wear
their many coloured coat, though I rarely
feel the cold and though it gets down
to minus seven here in the hills on the edge
of the vast expanding and contracting wheatplains,
ice on dam surfaces and windscreens quickly
shed as the sun lifts above the horizon
and past its false horizon, which is the coldest.
But, mostly, it burns here. Mostly the blood
boils and we pretend its illumination,
that painted ladies and spotted jezebels
and late in the piece the wanderers
promise a chrysalis architecture

to support the world as the world teeters
on the edge of total war – all those small
vicious and unbelievably cruel wars
linking up to alter the spread of sunlight,
disturb the flux of air, the flesh. And this
is all I have at any given time – lines to cast
out the facts and foil those "noble lies"
that keep the cultural profits flowing,
to evade their fangs and claws,
where country is turned to city
and bright boulevards
are the darkest alleyways
full of rubbish and the lost,
and the poor sleeping rough.
I lived on the streets on and off
over the years – decades back –
sleeping rough in the city's waste,
and the city was a petrified forest,
the city was the river held in check,
the city was the church that turned
a blind eye to the needle pricking the vein:
all that, in the eyes of God, all those
spirits pressed hard under the foundations
pushing up, calling out, breaking through.

JK

98.

"Love is invisible in this,
a texture lying in the bliss
and crude abyss that leads me
to lotus, sumac, and the wry
insoluble moment, a sly
design that my eye sets free."

— Jay Wright

John, I owe you this, a sloppy explaining,
sloppy because I am explaining effect
and not cause. I live these days
in a strange disquiet of love, finding myself,
as if for the first time, uncertain, nervous,
stomach heavy and hungry for a word like
saudade, which has no easy meaning, but
a mood we all think we know. It is
my same woman, Lorna, twenty-seven years in,
and yet I am a young man again, tender as earth
with a shallow water table – everything
uncertain, mad with jealousies and irrationalities.
My friends in Jamaica would warn
against the intrusion of slaughtered
roosters and crushed leaves and seeds;
a droplet perhaps of menstrual blood
and a scattering of light powder where
my feet normally walk. They'd say
there is reason and cause in this. I say "God"
to mean an unspeakable intimacy, the bounty
of forgiveness and grace, but that is private.
What I mean in poems is the unknowable
way of the future, or perhaps time's "big
picture" – I mean what will be left after
the destruction we know is upon us.

Three things have left me ill in the stomach
– a kind of indigestion – seething as I am about
the scowling Trump; this prophet's quarrel
with God; and love, returning to me
as delicious and as painful as it ever was,
but worse, for I thought the deal was that time
would make it easier, more certain. So this is
what I offer as a kind of clue to the signs
that you would have read across these pages,
the shadowing over all contemplations.
There are other themes, of course, but you
can see that death, illness, joy, good food,
impotence, fat, anger, money woes,
children, the broken earth, the geese,
and death again, time and time, those are
easily caught up in the heavy music
of these three themes, making what a man
translating my work called "una poesía que
se distancia para recuperarnos," meaning,
I think, that I make poems that seem distant,
and in their distance, they somehow rescue us;
which is lovely, except most of the time
I feel like the bewildered guide on a dark
road, unable to make out the signs on the highway.
Faith, then, in the rescue of words – words
that these days feel so capricious, so diabolic,
so inadequate. Let's call it faith.
Yes, I persist, friend. We do.

KD

99. Rusticus Eclogue

"'E's gwâin to leave his farm, as I da larn"

— William Barnes

Robert

All is aftermath
when you're on the losing end,
and they'll work extra hard to send
him down the harrowed path.

Thomas

To think they were childhood friends
in an isolated place, and now one sends
the other to the rails, and just to rub it in
offers to buy his old mate out, fuel the sin.

Robert

So what was their falling out?

Thomas

One grew GM canola and contaminated the organic crops of his
mate.

Robert

And now the victim will leave his farm?
And few will give a damn?
What of the rest of the shire?
What of the footy team and choir?

Thomas

The evil bastards Monsanto underwrote
the genetically enhanced substance abuse;
this was never going to be a case they'd lose –
no way they wanted a precedent, to quote
the law speaking to itself, caveat emptor
as a twisted specimen in legal trauma.

Robert

To tell the truth, *deep down* I've been wondering which way
to go myself... I mean, it's the way of things
now, aint it? The government's pushing
and we've got to keep up with technology.

Thomas

I am going to refuse their pressure;
trying to make us colonies of America –
make us plant what they want us to plant,
swamp the market so the market grants
benefits to those who comply –
I get sick of being dished out lie
after lie, I get sick of being in the thrall
of a mega corporation that makes us crawl,
wealthy shareholders who think they deserve
all the world has to offer up and more. They serve
those who own the seed and are served by them; they store
it up so we come crawling back for more. They claim to feed the poor!

Robert

Well, we're always being told what to do and how
to grow and then there's all this rights stuff,
you know, how we can and can't treat our stock – rough
handling, no mulesing, on and on they go.

183

And then there's the rubbish about meat
and health – my heart's as strong as an ox's! –
makes my head spin. I mean, some of these do-gooders love the fox
and the numbat – can't have both. A beer? My shout.

Thomas

Not now, mate – I'll take a rain check.
To tell the truth, I'm having a rethink
about how we got about our business.
I mean, the animals having feelings too – their stress
is our stress. And all these poisons we lavish on our paddocks,
they've gotta be affecting our kids. My boy can't concentrate in class.
Enough is enough. We've gotta make science serve us rather
than *us* serve science. I tell ya, I'm for the organic farmer.

Robert

I can't make head nor tail of it. But I do know that he'll be leaving
his farm
and his erstwhile mate has offered to buy him out. Victory works
like a charm.

Thomas

You can wax eloquent when you wanna, Bob, and you've not even
had a drink yet. Actually, I *will* have a beer with you – the crops are
strong and green!
It's a nasty business, this profit over friendship. Let's keep it in
perspective.

Robert

Too right, my friend. I am sorry he'll lose his farm but we've all gotta
live.

JK

184

100.

Were I better at this, I would study almanacs,
chart the seasons, visit Ted Kooser on his farm
in midwinter, without invitation, and carry his
two-by-fours and barbwire rolls to the edge of his
land, and ask him the names of the birds
turning in the sky, or the yield of the corn crop,
or the number of people he has buried – farm people,
his people. Were I better at this I would
drink coffee in the quaint cafes in western tiny
towns, talk to those wary of me at first.
By then I would have learned the dialect of cattle,
of waterways, of the market, and we could talk
of Coronation market in Kingston, where their produce
would sell, undercutting the machete-armed farmer
from St. Anne's organic yield, the world turning
into a biblical economy of famine and plenty.
I would be the inside man, the reporter, the one
to trace the secret incantation of chemicals,
how they translate into college fees, new trucks,
mortgages; this would be my labour, my art, even.

I am not a better man. Instead I make up stories
like one who has been promised that his sayings
will become the source of proverbs, and he will be
remembered as the lone man, hooded, walking
across the sea-hardened beach where the tide
has receded so far it appears a lie that soon
the bay will gleam with folds of the Atlantic;
who tells stories like this one about the woman
who one day, without warning, declares herself tired
of words, and leaves her family for a convent
where everyone stays silent and eats vegetables
and stews and artisan breads, and puts away
all devices that multiply words. She does this

for three weeks, pretending that she is tired
of speaking, but really is tired of hearing the sound
of her husband asking questions about heart
and fear and sorrow. So that when she returns
her depression is deeper, and she longs
for another month of empty silence, for
she has learnt that it is not so much words
she is escaping, but thought, the need
to make sense of things that have now
become too painful for thought. Of course,
she missed the beep of her phone, the friends
asking her where she is – that she missed.

And given the choice, wouldn't you choose
to be the guardian of the earth, instead of this
quite hapless chronicler of sorrows? There is a joke
here, and a proverb: "A man makes jokes
when he fears the joke is on him" – or something
such. Next time I will include a pot. I know
that these days comedians are sad. Why? Because,
they have the dull sorrow that makes funny
things unfunny, and no one beats a dead pan.

KD

101.

I am nothing in the story that unwinds without knowing it passed my
way — I called out but it didn't hear.

I am nothing if not the planting done when the moon is not
favourable, though I push out of red soil against the odds.

I am nothing because I lack a mythology and even my backstory is
broken up with the static of movement.

I am nothing if not the farmer who removes fences and watches the
wild animals pass through the paddocks.

I am nothing if not the encourager of birds in the furrows where they
can pick out unpoisoned seed.

I am nothing if not the harvester of wild greens that have grown on
stripped-back earth.

I am nothing but call and response through a valley that grows barer
by the year, hollower and hollower.

I am nothing but witness and resistance in which I call my name to
watch it vanish. Mistletoe birds keeping the records.

I am nothing but the wanderer who tries to settle down, though
knows the implications of staying. It is a dusty place.

I am nothing but the follower of voices of those I love, tracks clear
as an imprint left in mud, baked under a focused sun.

I am nothing but analogy and pathetic fallacy and overhearer of voices
that keep me awake when all seems still, quiet.

I am nothing but laughter ricocheting against the democratic choice of enclosure our neighbours deploy at election time.

I am nothing but the beach of an inland salt lake where pink crystals speak the myriad lives of algae and night parrots. Not extinct.

I am nothing but the recipient of your poems your prayers your invocations your songs your meditations your second sight.

JK

102.

As soon as we stepped through the gap
between the listing grey walls, the sky
darkened, the air chilled, and the birds
quarrelled. It is silent here in Luton,
in the grey and green of St. Mary's church,
in the cemetery where the dead who have done
their worst hum silently as bones.
In this sanctuary for ancient things,
the birds know to shelter here,
the rabbits abound, the soil is darkly
sumptuous. Maybe only in these
deep, green places, weather-worn stones,
uneven ground where the graves
break and settle, can one imagine
prayer and things lasting. I know
this is fantasy: the sky moves past,
the air is without discrimination, and holy
is just a prayer. Still, I imagine a day
spent on my back, asking an old verger
to repeat the names of the birds, the bushes,
the history of each stone, the stories
of a country that goes deep into the earth,
the catacombs of village after village,
the humility of the silent dead. There is here
a hint of what we might be. I will not
do this; it would spoil it all. This city
was built by the profit of sugar,
and we know the rest – the grand canker
that is interned with these bones,
in this sanctuary, in the vestry,
in the walls, in the trees. So much
remains, so much of what we bleed
into the ground remains, it seems,
and all peace is a moment of stillness,

without beginnings, without ends,
just the invention of a still point.
This peace is fleeting, a lie, a soft lie.

KD

103. Acknowledgement

for J & R

This is a bit of a tale. How should it be told?
In what order? Placing emphasis here, there?
It doesn't begin at the beginning, and its end
goes nowhere I can know, or need to know.
I was in the town of York yesterday. We go
there each Sunday to lunch with my mother
and her partner on the outskirts, under
the shades of Walwalinj, the wheatbelt
mountain. And from there I went into town
alone to look over an old building that had
been a store, then a private house, then
a backpackers' and now a gallery. The gallery
owners have restored it, as they did the old
Temple-Poole York post-office building,
colonial to its roots. In that building
I once rented a room where I wrote books
and read Spanish and Jewish poetry,
watched people pass in the street below.
So, I was talking with the couple who
run this new gallery, about how the town –
town implicated through my life –
has never acknowledged enough the brutal
theft of land from the Ballardong Noongar
people. That shootings, ear-cuttings – the full
range of "settler" cruelties and murder –
were the signatures of occupation.
And now, in that gallery, where local
Aboriginal art will soon be speaking
its truths from the walls, through the walls,
"history" might find its many voices.
Strange thing is that I recognised a corridor

191

of that building from way back into
my childhood. Maybe I visited
with my auntie after church to collect
something, to hand something over.
Maybe it was a brief moment of farm-talk.
I can't piece it together, this fragmented
story, underwritten with the utterances
of all that would be written over, pushed down,
but will always, to the core of earth itself,
speak its people, reclaiming all that settlers
would have them lose – and all that the modern
settler-apologists would have as status quo.
From up in that office in the thick-walled
post-office building, I never studied
people's faces, only the swift and slow
movements of their feet. Even then,
a decade ago, I knew something
was afoot. And I waited. And waited.
Hoping acknowledgement
will be made in full.

JK

104.

When we began I was thinking so much of guns
and the damage they cause, and the bodies
they break, and the world dismantling
around us. It has only been a few months
and it is not as if anything has changed,
but now I am thinking of the quarrels
and conspiracies and fictions and fears
in my head, it is strange to me how deeply
those shadows follow each day. The dreams
I have during half sleep – the minutes
between the alarm and rising – are novels,
truly, and have a taste in them that covers
the day. By this, I mean, I am haunted
by my inventions. So what of the Nigerian
in the tube? He's chasing leggings-wearing,
jewelled girls, giggling and fearful: "Don't
be afraid of me, I am not a molester
of women. Are you afraid of a black man?"
He is drinking a bottle of red wine. We try
not to make eye contact, but he wants to talk.
I know the things in his head are following
him, consuming him. "Oyibo!" he barks
at a white man minding his own business,
"I am a sixty-four-year-old man, what can
you say to me. I am a mechanical engineer.
I have a job – what do you have to say to me?"
The blows are all scattered, the man
punching and missing, the attacked sober
and able to avoid the swings. "I am celebrating,
celebrating. Thirty years in this country;
I worked here, worked here." He is in jeans,
an open, loose cotton shirt, dragging a roller
bag. Going or coming, he is travelling light.
"Jesus, ahh, Jesus is the light, yes,

ha, light. I am celebrating. Prostate cancer,
and Dr. Green at Manchester Hospital said,
'You are better now, healed!' Jesus. I am
healed, me, Nigerian. You go to my country,
and oil, oil, oil, and we can't even keep
the fucking lights on! The last time
I was there was in 1980. Can't keep a fucking
light on. And I am working in your country."
We leave him there, shades on his forehead,
head bobbing. It is like one of those
dreams repeated and repeated, and I think
I understand him, the walking fear – and I envy him
that in the morning he will have forgotten.
Still, I regret my scowl; my Lorna's softer
face made him say, "Madam, madam,"
as if appealing to the more reasonable justice.
It is enough to make me wonder
at the noises I am walking with these days.
Now, every single body I have eulogised
is this tall Nigerian man, in sandals, loose
jeans, unsteady, carrying in his body
so many histories, and in just these slivers
of light, we encounter something that will last.

KD

105.

Yes, almost… and yet only ten months have passed
since this new beginning, since setting the clocks back.
Or forward. Today, we went out to Oak Park
which I wrote about a couple of years ago,
which I wrote about as a gentle shock to the system,
but this time it wasn't displays of fertility but the burning-
off of the wheatbelt. Floods in the heat of January
followed by intense dry, and the legalised firebugs
are burning their farms to the dirt – stubble
and chaff the excuse to burn out great trees
whose shade has bothered the crops,
to let flames run riot into the three percent
of bush that's left. In summer, locals fight fires,
in autumn, they burn everything down below
the plimsoll line. As I write, I watch flames
thirty-feet high across the valley, torching
the glassy remnants of a wheatcrop; farmers
"can't do much about" the flames reaching up
into the canopies of wandoos and York gums…
The prescribed is the annihilation of habitat.
The prescribed is the bumper harvest before famine.
But at Oak Park itself, lake of dead trees – rusted
metal sculpture of settlement, the pioneering way –
place sacred to local Noongar people, their once "supermarket"*
without big guys siphoning off the profits, surrounded
by farms burning burning burning – but at Oak Park
the power of red morrels shedding their bark,
the golden whistler's prophecy and declarations,
the swamp oaks holding the edges in place,
the mother teal on salty water in a granite cradle
instructing her ducklings, the kangaroo prints
on the sandy track, the gnamma holes

_____

* As described to me by a number of Noongar elders over the years.

195

aching water against the dry and smoke,
the carbon bonanza that will spread to the world,
the port lincoln parrots which Tracy says
are greener here than anywhere,
and Tim, documenting, documenting,
our voices – all our voices – part of the soundtrack.
And home now, home, watching the flames,
the smoke so thick it makes war on the sky,
the birds – all the birds – flying away,
flying from smoke plume to smoke plume,
even the low-flying birds reaching
so high their wings drop off…
Yes, almost… and yet only ten months have passed
since this new beginning, since setting the clocks back.
Or forward. And today we went out to Oak Park.

JK

106.

"So it was we came to red sky
country, flame red were flame
red, blood red. Stylised fire
flared

everywhere, red flame water-

colour brush tip, brush blood
mixed with water…"

— Nathaniel Mackey, "Departure from Troy"

There is in me a lust for the chronicler's language;
the rhetoric of the one who moves with a tribe,
who writes of the march of the congregation
over hostile land, the stories of the births
and the deaths, the legends of our stores,
where water will be found, what squats
on the other side of a mountain, waiting.
Mostly the chronicler looks back at the detritus
left behind by travelers, the discards, the carelessly
abandoned; the chronicler brings up the rear
where those who are either too occupied
with the present – dreams, loves, regrets –
form the straggling mob, filled with the sounds
of all extremes: deepest silence, groans and giggles,
and the dry, breathless wail of loss. The one
who writes the story of the tribe lives
among those who have lost the most and those
who have gained the most, and this is what
she will write, knowing full well that these words,
this account that maps the new territory
by what is left behind, will not be called

the history of a people, but the deep song,
the myth, the faith, the spirit of the tribe.
I envy the shadowy troubadour's soft voice
curling through the stretches of verse behind
us, and I, returning to that music, am at once
lost and discovered, full of heaviness
and elation – the epiphany of a sliver
of beauty: "light like a feather, heavy as lead".
To be clear, I am envying the selves we have
made in this music we have shared all these months,
where we step high through the long grasses
of the open prairie, where ancient bones
still jut out of the earth, where the sun
will spark a glint of light – leading us to the trace
of what is left behind, and quickly, we write it down.

There's a reward for me

There's a reward for me

KD

107.

"Music's where had evaded us, elsewhere's
elsewhere."

— Nathaniel Mackey ("Lullaby in Lagos")

(i)

There are no tribes for me – I am an outcast
by design and default. Which is not to say
I wouldn't welcome being called into the circle,
or that I don't respect the circle. I do I do I do.

But I stare too long into the shadows, the foliage
as it is dragged away from the periphery. Here –
no there, there I am. And I the music, and I huddling
up to catch the tales and weave snippets

into the blanket of night I secure against the cold.
But mostly I don't feel the cold – I agitate
in thyrotoxicosis and live somewhere between
bird and human, sticking stars up into a blank

sky, equating memory with gravity drawing
me in and in to the vortex of utterances.
To speak before you can walk, and walk early.
To obsess over fate in Aeschylus and Hardy.

(ii)

My recovery is Django Reinhardt and Stéphane
Grappelli. It is Django turning physical impairment
to a new music. Part of the puzzle of hot jazz.

And aircraft carriers are playing their gambits.
And volley ball is played over a testing site,
deep below. The secretive regime. Area 51.

We slide through the variations, and a rufous
whistler male reterritorialises after an absence.
It's not easy loving on the molecular level –

every particle that makes up friends and enemies.
To love them all, even as you recoil in horror.
We let rooms close in to make a vision of outdoors.

The guitar and violin enlivening melancholy.
But I'll survive even if one leaf – air parsing
its paper – speaks up. My body discarded.

(iii)

I've tried to enter war zones thinking I could stop
the fighting, or at least one bullet from finding
its mark. Or catch shrapnel. In this delusion
I grew exasperated, held back. By others,
myself. Decades ago. And now, I send these
peace offerings no one will take me up on,
hoping they'll stop a bullet in someone's
heart's pocket. Tombs I am already
divided across, the odour of strong bulbs
sprouting at their doors. Or the nameless
fertilisation of soil so over-fertilised
nothing can grow, in the ever or again.
In the same way, when I was in my late teens,
I preferred language that didn't work,
translations that didn't add up. All of it
piecemeal, all of it contrived into shape.

(iv)

It won't do if I just say what happens?
I ask the passers-by, leaning heavily
against the shadows. And there's a tune
to follow in a roundabout way, back
to the long sharp blades of green grass
at the base of the tree: a flat-top yates.

All the places are mixed up, muddled
together. A Painted Jezebel butterfly
tells me the reason contemporary
(it staggers this across even more
syllables than it possesses) poets
refer to poetry and poets so often

in their verse(s), is because they fear
irrelevancy and redundancy and being
separated from the tribes. They fear
their own buying power, though won't
renounce, no never renounce. No
never renounce entirely renounce.

Not for an ounce of quiddity or an ounce
of high. And so they still, they still
worship the sky, sky thick to the touch.

(v)

The music was lost because it got
written out somehow in the rewrite
a collaborative gesture that took
séga and maloya and rolled them

into one riff on the sea on reef,
one shark sailing between the east

coast of Africa and La Réunion,
such different moods, messages;

and I was there and the trauma
resonated through the canefields
and over the black lavatic rocks
and the bats flew crazy with evening.

No, not lost, written out because
the rhythm is barely translated
the rhythm is barely a remainder
in the tossing onto the shipwreck

coast. And now I am thinking
that way, heading that way,
to the creole and animism,
to whatever it is I see

from the heights, looking
down into the cirques,
smelling the volcano's
sulphur wreathing

the globe, for it reaches
us here, inland, on the edge
of the hills where night's contract
is a for a sunset that is neither

darkness nor light,
sad and resplendent.

JK

108.

Coda

Before the silence, then,
Django Reinhardt's sensual speed searching for his nomadic tribe:
"I Saw Stars" – yes, thick to the touch;

Nina Simone's patience with open spaces of silence:
"My Man Gone Now"– so many things slipping away,
leaving us with the thick beauty of silence;

Bob Marley fading away with his plaintive plea
"It's not true, it's not true…"
Yuh running and yuh running and yuh running away…

KD

END

ABOUT THE AUTHORS

Kwame Dawes is the author of over thirty books, and is widely recognised as one of the Caribbean's leading authors. He is the Glenna Luschei Editor of *Prairie Schooner* and a Chancellor's Professor of English at the University of Nebraska. His latest book with Northwestern University Press and Peepal Tree is *City of Bones: A Testament*. His third book of poetry, *Prophets* (1995), is republished this year with a *Reader's Guide*. He was born in Ghana, grew up in Jamaica and has lived most of his adult life in the USA.

John Kinsella's many books of poetry include *Armour* (Picador, 2010), *Jam Tree Gully* (WW Norton, 2012) and *Drowning in Wheat: Selected Poems* (Picador, 2016). His newest collection, from Arc Publications, is *The Wound*. He has published work in all genres and across a few of them as well, and collaborated with many artists, composers, writers and poets. He is a fellow of Churchill College, Cambridge University, and Professor of Literature and Environment at Curtin University in Western Australia.

ALSO BY KWAME DAWES AND JOHN KINSELLA

Speak from Here to There
ISBN: 9781845233198; pp. 243; pub. 2016; £9.99

Kwame Dawes' base was the flat prairieland of Lincoln, Nebraska, a landscape in which he, a black man, originally from Ghana and Jamaica, felt at once alien and deeply committed to the challenges of finding "home". John Kinsella's base was in the violently beautiful landscape of Western Australia, his home ground, thick with memory and the challenge of ecological threat and political ineptitude. In the first cycle, Echoes and Refrains, the poets sought and found a language for this conversation of various modes and moods. They were linked by the political and social upheavals in their respective spheres – Dawes contemplating the waves of violence consuming the US and the world, and Kinsella confronting the injustice of the theft of indigenous land and the terrible treatment of refugees and immigrants. These poems chart an unpredictable journey towards friendship. They reflect commonalities – love of family, cricket, art, politics, music, and travel – and in poem after poem one senses how each is hungry to hear from the other and to then treat the revelations that arrive as triggers for his own lyric introspection – risky, complex, formally considered and beautiful. They stretch one another, and provoke to a poetic honesty that comes with authority and assurance. In the second cycle of poems, Illuminations, locations shift but the concerns remain and are considered in different lights. *Speak from Here to There* reminds us of how poetry can offer comfort and solace, and how it can ignite the peculiar creative frenzy that enriches us.